COMMON SENSE
QUESTIONS ABOUT
SCHOOL ADMINISTRATION

OTHER BOOKS BY GERARD GIORDANO

Commonsense Questions about Instruction: The Answers Can Provide Essential Steps to Improvement (2014)

Capping Costs: Putting a Price Tag on School Reform (2012)

Teachers Go to Rehab: Historical and Current Advice to Instructors (2012)

Lopsided Schools: Case Method Briefings (2011)

Cockeyed Education: A Case Method Primer (2010)

Solving Education's Problems Effectively: A Guide to Using the Case Method (2009)

COMMON SENSE QUESTIONS ABOUT SCHOOL ADMINISTRATION

The Answers Can Provide Essential Steps to Improvement

Gerard Giordano

ROWMAN & LITTLEFIELD
Lanham • Boulder • New York • London

Published by Rowman & Littlefield
A wholly owned subsidiary of
The Rowman & Littlefield Publishing Group, Inc.
4501 Forbes Boulevard, Suite 200, Lanham, Maryland 20706
www.rowman.com

Unit A, Whitacre Mews, 26-34 Stannary Street, London SE11 4AB

Copyright © 2015 by Gerard Giordano

All rights reserved. No part of this book may be reproduced in any form or by any electronic or mechanical means, including information storage and retrieval systems, without written permission from the publisher, except by a reviewer who may quote passages in a review.

British Library Cataloguing in Publication Information Available

Library of Congress Cataloging-in-Publication Data

Giordano, Gerard, 1946–
  Common sense questions about school administration : the answers can provide essential steps to improvement / Gerard Giordano.
    pages cm
  Includes bibliographical references.
  ISBN 978-1-4758-1261-9
  1.   School management and organization. 2. Educational leadership. I. Title.
LB2805+ 2015

2014043284

DEDICATION

This book, which is based on dialogues with my students, is dedicated to them.

CONTENTS

Tables	ix
Acknowledgment	xiii
Preface: Do Principals Ignore Common Sense Questions?	xv
1 Do Questions Always Require Answers?	1
2 Does Analytics Belong in Schools?	15
3 Does For-Profit Ideology Make Sense in Public Education?	27
4 Can School Leaders Get Some Things for Nothing?	41
5 How Are Educational Questions Framed?	53
6 Do Charter Schools Improve Public Education?	67
7 What Is the Secret behind Accurate Predictions?	79
8 Are Textbooks Political?	91
9 How Should Principals Be Recruited?	103
10 Can Simple Solutions Eliminate Complex Problems?	115
References	127
About the Author	153

TABLES

1.1	Law School Administrators Pose a Hypophoric Question about Lawyers	8
1.2	A School Critic Poses a Hypophoric Question about Test Scores	9
1.3	A School Critic Poses a Rhetorical Question about Teachers Unions	10
1.4	A Union Proponent Poses a Hypophoric Question about National Standards	11
1.5	Union Proponents Pose a Rhetorical Question about Teacher Accountability	12
2.1	A Baseball Manager Uses Analytics during Losing Streaks	22
2.2	A Baseball Manager Uses Analytics during Winning Streaks	23
2.3	The Chicago School Board Uses Analytics to Restrict Teachers' Salaries	24
2.4	The Chicago School Board Uses Analytics to Close Schools	25
3.1	Entrepreneurs Engage in Patent Trolling	37

3.2	Entrepreneurs Establish For-Profit Schools	38
3.3	Entrepreneurs Collaborate with the Florida Virtual School	39
4.1	Delta Uses Customer Relations	49
4.2	Principals Use Customer Relations	50
4.3	A Superintendent Uses Customer Relations	51
5.1	A Retailer Frames Products	60
5.2	Politicians Frame Legislation and Litigation	61
5.3	A President Frames Gun Control Legislation	62
5.4	Educators Frame School Safety Procedures	63
5.5	Entrepreneurs Frame Safety-Related School Equipment	64
6.1	A Philanthropist Poses Questions about Bowdoin College	74
6.2	A President Refuses to Answer Questions about Bowdoin College	75
6.3	Florida Teachers Pose Questions about Charter Schools	76
6.4	Florida Politicians Refuse to Answer Questions about Charter Schools	77
7.1	A Fox News Pollster Makes Political Predictions	85
7.2	A *New York Times* Pollster Makes Political Predictions	86
7.3	Assessment Experts Make Predictions about STAAR	87
7.4	Texas Teachers Make Predictions about STAAR	88
8.1	An Investor Sells Herbalife Stocks Short	97
8.2	Investors Sell Herbalife Stocks Long	98
8.3	Publishers Align Textbooks with American Exceptionalism	99
8.4	Publishers Align Textbooks with the Common Core	100
9.1	Corporate Boards Offer Enormous Bonuses	110
9.2	Corporate Boards Offer Generous Severance Packages	111

9.3	School Boards Offer Modest Bonuses	112
9.4	School Boards Offer Administrative Tenure	113
10.1	Enthusiasts Recommend Fallout Shelters	121
10.2	Enthusiasts Recommend Race-Based School Calendars	122
10.3	Enthusiasts Recommend Extended School Calendars for Students with Disabilities	123
10.4	Enthusiasts Recommend Extended School Calendars for All Students	124

ACKNOWLEDGMENT

Like all of my recent books, this one is a collaborative effort with my superlative editor, Tom Koerner.

PREFACE

Do Principals Ignore Common Sense Questions?

How can student learning be assessed?

—Linda Suskie, 2009

What are the major obstacles facing education . . . analytics?

—Audrey Watters, 2011

Great teachers lead to successful students . . . but what about . . . principals?

—"Highly Effective," 2012

Should parents [rather than principals] . . . pull the trigger on schools?

—Mary McConnell, 2012

Should principals . . . be armed?

—"Daily Poll," 2012

Would you return . . . school discipline . . . to building principals?

—"John Liu on Education," 2013

> What do we know about . . . principal evaluation?
>
> —Susanna Loeb & Jason Grissom, 2013

> [Are] for-profits . . . [an] aid or vice in public education?
>
> —Michael Horn, 2013

> Is it too hard [for principals] to get rid of an incompetent teacher now?
>
> —Susan Page, 2014

> How common is [administrator] cheating on [high-stakes] tests?
>
> —Anya Kamenetz, 2014

> Why are teachers unions so opposed to change?
>
> —Antonio Villaraigosa, former mayor, 2014

Mayors and principals have well-defined responsibilities. They can be defiant when they are questioned about the manner in which they discharge them.

A DEFIANT MAYOR

Michael Bloomberg was a candidate for mayor of New York City in 2001. He had traits that made him stand out from other candidates: he was poised, organized, impeccably dressed, photogenic, articulate, and media savvy.

Bloomberg had another trait that made him stand out. He was remarkably affluent; he managed a twenty-five-billion-dollar fortune.

Bloomberg anticipated that his wealth would endear him to rich and influential constituents. However, he worried that it would alienate him from those who were poor and powerless.

Bloomberg entreated all residents to support him. He stated that he truly understood their plight. He pledged to create civic programs that would help everyone.

After he won the election, Bloomberg did devise numerous programs. Nonetheless, he realized that they were ignored by most citizens. He hoped to attract their attention with an initiative to foster nutritious diets.

Some residents had confidence in Bloomberg's dietary campaign. However, others were skeptical. Many local journalists suspected that the mayor had ulterior motives (Dwyer, 2013).

The journalists wondered whether Bloomberg personally followed his own dietary advice. They asked him if he was avoiding heavily salted foods. They were disappointed when he defiantly dodged the question.

The journalists looked for an unconventional way to get an answer. They followed the mayor and secretly observed the food that he ordered in restaurants. They discovered that he not only selected high-sodium items but then sprinkled extra salt onto them. They gleefully shared their discovery with the public (Barbaro, 2009; Rovzar, 2009; Sullum, 2009).

DEFIANT PRINCIPALS

Parents have questions about schools. Many of them try to get answers from principals. Parents go to principals because they are accessible.

Parents have another reason to go to principals. They realize that they are accountable for virtually every aspect of the schools.

Principals are responsible for educational facilities. They manage laboratories, gymnasiums, green spaces, parking lots, restrooms, cafeterias, outdoor athletic sites, recital halls, theaters, and the special accommodations for children with disabilities.

Principals are responsible for learning materials. They influence the selection of equipment that can range from textbooks to sports gear.

Principals are responsible for personnel. They hire, retain, and reward teachers, professionals, and auxiliary workers.

Principals are responsible for budgets. They allocate the funds for administrative, instructional, and extracurricular activities.

Principals are responsible for school safety. They ensure that students, staff, and property are protected.

Parents concede that principals make multiple decisions. Nonetheless, they suspect that principals sometimes have ulterior motives. They ask principals to identify specific instances in which they have improved schools. Parents insist that they are posing a common sense question.

The parents are annoyed when principals give artful responses; they assume that the principals are insincere. They are furious when principals give no response; they assume that the principals are defiant.

Some of the parents try to get an answer from superintendents and school board members. Others are less conventional. They implore journalists, businesspeople, and politicians to help them get an answer.

THIS BOOK

This book is special. It is original, practical, and filled with engrossing examples. It is special for several additional reasons.

This book presents stimulating comments at the beginning of each chapter. These comments highlight the key issues in the chapter. Those at the beginning of this preface highlight issues that recur throughout the entire book.

This book incorporates a distinctive approach to problem solving: the case method. Readers use the case method to identify important questions, the formats in which they are posed, the motives of the groups that pose them, the answers that they elicit, and the educational changes that they trigger.

This book contains unique exercises. These exercises model the dialogues that transpire in case-based seminars. The exercises can be completed by groups that actually are enrolled in seminars. They also can be completed by individuals who are reading this book on their own but who wish to simulate the dialogues in seminars.

This book is intended for professionals who work directly in the schools: administrators, teachers, and guidance counselors. It also is intended for persons who interact indirectly with schools: parents, politicians, school board members, university students, and professors.

This book, which focuses on school administrators, is part of a series. The first book concentrated on teachers. Subsequent volumes will concentrate on tests and students.

1

DO QUESTIONS ALWAYS REQUIRE ANSWERS?

Rhetorical . . . questions . . . convey assertions.

—Irene Koshik, 2005

What is stopping us from changing [our schools]?

—Mayor Antonio Villaraigosa, quoted by Childs, 2011

Is closing schools . . . so teachers can . . . protest . . . the best way . . . [of] serving children?

—Andrew Rotherham, 2011

[Are standardized] tests . . . truly aligned with the curriculum?

—Susan Schultz, quoted by Smith, 2012

How does lowering educational standards prepare kids for . . . college?

—Robert Small, quoted in "Maryland Police," 2013

Why would you write a blank check to your neighborhood school?

—Dave Hodges, 2013

Why don't [Bill Gates's] children attend schools with increased class sizes?

—"Dear Bill," 2013

Is Common Core really state-led?

—Todd Thurman, 2014

If more money was [sic] the answer, wouldn't [reading] be much higher?

—Edwin Feulner, 2014

Language is used for all sorts of reasons other than to convey thought accurately.

—Barton Swaim, 2014

Groups *do not always pose questions to elicit information. They sometimes have ulterior motives.*

LAW SCHOOL ADMINISTRATORS

Countless events influenced the course of politics during the second half of the twentieth century. Nonetheless, few of them had greater impact than the Watergate break-in and cover-up.

Journalists provided the public with details about the roles of key Watergate figures, many of whom were prominent lawyers. They then asked who should be blamed for the key figures' deplorable behavior (Curriden, 2012; Fisher, 2012).

University administrators realized that they prepared lawyers. They were disconcerted when journalists asked questions about immoral lawyers. They were even more disconcerted when readers, listeners, and viewers echoed the questions.

The university administrators repeated the questions about immoral lawyers. They then responded that they would take some of the blame. They explained that they were responsible because they failed to make all law candidates study ethics (Gillers, 2012).

The administrators vowed to expand lawyer-training curricula with mandatory ethics courses. They hoped that this response would appease critics. They hoped it also would generate tuition (Dean & Robenalt, 2012; Rigertasal, 2012).

CRITICS OF PUBLIC SCHOOLS

When university administrators were under pressure, they employed *hypophora*. They posed questions and immediately provided self-serving answers (Zimmer, 2012).

People were impressed with hypophora. They detected its persuasive power. People who had been criticizing the public schools were particularly impressed.

Hypophoric Questions

School critics were concerned about numerous educational problems. In particular, they fretted over test scores. They blamed teachers when the scores were low.

The critics claimed that unionized teachers paid too little attention to their students' academic needs. Critics chastised teachers for concentrating on their own financial needs. They urged teachers to reverse their priorities.

The critics had a proposal to force teachers to pay more attention to students. They would make high test scores the conditions for bonuses, salary increases, and job retention. They waited to see how the teachers would respond.

The critics were not surprised when the teachers were cool to their proposal. They judged that teachers were unenthusiastic because they had conflicts of interest. Critics decided to use hypophoric questions to underscore teachers' conflicts (Baker, 2012; "Principles," 2013; Zernike, 2012).

One California critic was upset because a local school district did not have the funds to cover all of its operating expenses. He fumed when the district received a special state allocation. He asked who had benefited. He immediately answered that unionized teachers were the sole beneficiaries ("Jerry Brown's School Bailout," 2012).

Another critic asked why public-school teachers were not being punished when their students earned low scores on tests. She answered her own question, stating that the teachers could not be punished because of the protection that they received from powerful unions (Kenny, 2012).

Critics made hypophoric questions into the titles of books. One of them selected the title, *Who's Ruining our Schools?* He supplied the answer in the subtitle: *The Case against the NEA Teacher Union* (Alexander, 1988).

When school critics used hypophoric questions, they did not believe that they were changing the minds of unionized teachers. However, they did believe that they might be changing the minds of parents.

Rhetorical Questions

When people pose questions, they do not always expect responses to them. They do not expect responses when they accompany their questions with answers. They also do not expect them when their questions are rhetorical.

Rhetorical questions have common sense answers. For example, a question about whether the sky is blue has an obvious answer ("Rhetorical Questions," 2013).

School critics were fascinated by rhetorical questions. They judged that they could be extremely persuasive. They made them into the titles for their books.

One school critic wished to make it clear that the mission of schools was distinct from that of teachers unions. He made this point in his book's title: *Conflicting Missions?* He assumed that his question had an obvious, common sense answer (Loveless, 2000).

Bobby Jindal, the governor of Louisiana, admired nonunionized teachers because they worked for low wages. He asked whether the state should reward the schools that hired them. He assumed this question had a common sense answer (Williams, 2012).

Jindal admired another group: parents who sent their children to private schools. He explained that the state would have to spend more on education if these parents were to send their children to public schools. He used a rhetorical question to make this point. He asked whether the state should reimburse the parents for the money they spent on private-school tuition. He assumed that the question had a common sense answer (Williams, 2012).

School critics used rhetorical questions to show their displeasure with unionized teachers. They did not believe that they were changing the minds of those teachers. However, they did believe that they might be changing the minds of parents.

ADVOCATES OF PUBLIC SCHOOLS

Unionized teachers were upset by challenges from critics. They hoped the leaders of their labor organizations would deflect those challenges (Giordano, 2012a, 2012b; Davey & Greenhouse, 2012).

Hypophoric Questions

Although union proponents may have been upset with the allegations that critics made, they were impressed with the persuasive strategies that the critics employed and, in fact, resolved to adopt their strategies.

One union leader was irate after critics characterized national educational standards as antidotes for incompetent teachers. She posed a hypophoric question: she asked whether the standards would "sing" in classrooms. She immediately answered that they would "sing" only if they were bolstered by additional funds for schools (Rich, 2012).

Union proponents posed hypophoric questions about how teachers should be evaluated. They responded that teachers should be evaluated with complex procedures like those used in nations with exemplary schools (Darling-Hammond, 2012; Sahlberg, 2011).

Union proponents made hypophoric questions into book titles. Several authors selected the title, *School Effectiveness for Whom?* They then supplied the answer in a subtitle: *Challenges to the School Effectiveness and School Improvement Movements* (Slee, Weiner, & Tomlinson, 1998).

When union proponents used hypophoric questions, they did not believe that they were changing the minds of school critics. However, they did believe that they might be changing the minds of parents.

Rhetorical Questions

Union proponents were impressed by the power of rhetorical questions. They looked for opportunities to use them.

Union proponents made rhetorical questions into the titles of books. Several authors needed a title for a book about several school initiatives that they opposed. They chose the title, *Retrenchment or Reform?* (Henderson, Urban, & Wolman, 2004).

Dianne Ravitch was a pugnacious union critic. However, she later became an ardent union advocate. She posed rhetorical questions during both ideological phases.

When she was a union critic, Ravitch (2003) decried the liberal political groups that endorsed "anti-bias and sensitivity guidelines." She asked, *Can We Stop Them?* She assumed that anti-union readers would know the common sense answer to this question.

Ravitch (2012) later decried the conservative political groups that were attacking unions. She blamed them for privatizing, closing, and restaffing schools. She asked, "Do you know of any high-performing nation in the world that got that way by privatizing public schools, closing those with low test scores, and firing teachers?" At this time, she was writing for pro-union readers. She assumed that they would know the common sense answer to her question.

When union proponents posed rhetorical questions, they did not believe that they were changing the minds of school critics. However, they did believe that they might be changing the minds of parents.

CASE METHOD

Five case-method activities are presented at the end of this chapter. They highlight instances in which questions were used to persuade listeners rather than elicit information from them.

Case-method activities are used rarely in the field of teacher education. However, they are used extensively in legal education. Law professors introduce their students to case-method strategies in university lecture halls. They hope that they eventually will apply them in courtrooms.

Teacher educators can encourage their students to apply case-method strategies to simulated scholastic problems. Their students later may apply those strategies to actual scholastic problems (Giordano, 2009, 2010, 2011, 2012b).

EXAMINING PERSUASIVE QUESTIONS

Questions do not always require answers. They do not require them when the answers are self-evident; they do not require them when the answers are attached to them.

Activity 1.1

Law school administrators asked why lawyers behaved deplorably. They then answered their own question: lawyers required ethics courses. How did groups respond?

Table 1.1 identifies two groups: journalists and their audiences.

Complete the table by indicating the ways in which the groups responded to the law school administrators. You can use symbols.

Use the symbol − if the groups exhibited low interest. Use the symbol ± for moderate interest and the symbol + for high interest. As a final step, explain the bases for the symbols that you selected.

You can rely on the information in this chapter, additional information, or the information cited in the references. If you are reading this chapter with colleagues, you can confer with them.

Table 1.1. Law School Administrators Pose a Hypophoric Question about Lawyers

Groups	Response*	Explanation
Journalists		
Audiences		

*− Low
± Moderate
+ High

Activity 1.2

A school critic asked why teachers were not punished for students' low test scores. She then answered her own question: teachers were protected by unions. How did groups respond?

DO QUESTIONS ALWAYS REQUIRE ANSWERS?

Table 1.2 identifies two groups: unionized teachers and parents.

Complete the table by indicating the ways in which the groups responded to the school critic. You can use symbols.

Use the symbol – if the groups exhibited low interest. Use the symbol ± for moderate interest and the symbol + for high interest. As a final step, explain the bases for the symbols that you selected.

Table 1.2. A School Critic Poses a Hypophoric Question about Test Scores

Groups	Response*	Explanation
Unionized Teachers		
Parents		

*– Low
± Moderate
+ High

Activity 1.3

A school critic asked whether teachers unions and school reformers had conflicting missions. He did not think the question required an answer; he assumed that it had a self-evident, common sense answer. How did groups respond?

Table 1.3 identifies two groups: unionized teachers and parents.

Complete the table by indicating the ways in which the groups responded to the school critic. You can use symbols.

Use the symbol – if the groups exhibited low interest. Use the symbol ± for moderate interest and the symbol + for high interest. As a final step, explain the bases for the symbols that you selected.

Table 1.3. A School Critic Poses a Rhetorical Question about Teachers Unions

Groups	Response*	Explanation
Unionized Teachers		
Parents		

*– Low
± Moderate
+ High

DO QUESTIONS ALWAYS REQUIRE ANSWERS?

Activity 1.4

A union proponent asked whether national standards would "sing." She then answered her own question: they would "sing" only if they were accompanied by funds. How did groups respond?

Table 1.4 identifies two groups: school critics and parents.

Complete the table by indicating the ways in which the groups responded to the union proponent. You can use symbols.

Use the symbol – if the groups exhibited low interest. Use the symbol ± for moderate interest and the symbol + for high interest. As a final step, explain the bases for the symbols that you selected.

Table 1.4. A Union Proponent Poses a Hypophoric Question about National Standards

Groups	Response*	Explanation
School Critics		
Parents		

*– Low
± Moderate
+ High

Activity 1.5

Union proponents asked whether teacher accountability measures should be viewed as retrenchment or reform. They did not think the question required an answer; they assumed that it had a self-evident, common sense answer. How did groups respond?

Table 1.5 identifies two groups: school critics and parents.

Complete the table by indicating the ways in which the groups responded to the union proponents. You can use symbols.

Use the symbol − if the groups exhibited low interest. Use the symbol ± for moderate interest and the symbol + for high interest. As a final step, explain the bases for the symbols that you selected.

Table 1.5. Union Proponents Pose a Rhetorical Question about Teacher Accountability

Groups	Response*	Explanation
School Critics		
Parents		

*− Low
± Moderate
+ High

SUMMARY

Questions do not always require answers. They sometimes are hypophoric: they are accompanied by answers. They sometimes are rhetorical: they have self-evident answers.

2

DOES ANALYTICS BELONG IN SCHOOLS?

Are big data approaches the answer to K12 educational [problems]?

—Christopher Dawson, 2012

K–12 schools . . . are drowning in data.

—Center for Digital Education, 2013

Analytics are needed in the education market.

—Jay Liebowitz, 2013

Analytics . . . is . . . promising to . . . transform education.

—"Will Analytics," 2013

[Analytics can] help administrators . . . make better decisions.

—"Education Analytics," 2013

Schools should . . . have data-driven . . . systems.

—"A Better Approach," 2014

Sports managers and business leaders used analytics to help them with difficult decisions. They made an impression on school administrators.

SPORTS ANALYTICS

Late twentieth-century businesspeople had to make critical decisions; they frequently relied on personal intuitions.

The businesspeople wished to improve their decision making. Worried that they were relying excessively on intuitions, they decided to statistically analyze data. Referring to this approach as analytics, they applied it to banking, finance, manufacturing, marketing, real estate, logistics, and retailing (Aggarwal, 2011; Davenport & Harris, 2007; Hirshleifer & Riley, 1992).

Businesspeople had opportunities to discover analytics from their professional peers. Nonetheless, many of them learned about it from the manager of the Oakland Athletics (Lewis, 2003; Miller et al., 2012).

The owners of the Oakland Athletics were upset about the number of games that their baseball team was winning. They hired Billy Beane as manager. They told him to make changes.

Beane realized that professional baseball managers made a common assumption. They assumed that the amount they spent on players' salaries determined the number of games that they would win. Beane referred to this conviction as *moneyball*.

Beane had a relatively modest budget. He could not fill his roster with high-priced players. In fact, he had difficulty retaining all of his current high-priced players. He needed an alternative to *moneyball*.

Beane asked an analytics expert to compile data on current baseball players. He wanted to identify the players who were paid little but who still were able to get on base. He hoped that these players would be able to compete with the league's high-salaried stars.

Beane used the analytics data to reconfigure his team. He was depressed when the team initially struggled to win games. However, he was elated as it later became more and more competitive.

Oakland's sports journalists were fascinated by analytics. When the team was losing games, they disapproved of it. When it was winning games, they approved. They had an influence on fans, who responded to analytics in the same fashion.

The Oakland players reacted predictably to analytics. The high-salaried players who lost jobs scoffed at it; the low-salaried players who obtained jobs praised it.

The managers of many baseball teams were impressed by Oakland's use of analytics. In fact, coaches from multiple sports were impressed. Some of them used analytics to win games; others used it to rationalize controversial decisions (Alamar, 2013; Alamar & Mehrotra, 2012).

EDUCATIONAL ANALYTICS

Mayors, superintendents, and school boards were educational leaders; they were responsible for the schools in their communities. They frequently set ambitious and expensive-to-achieve goals. They realized that they needed money to succeed.

The educational leaders were pragmatic. When they did not have enough money to achieve their goals, they shifted funds from one budgetary category to another. They looked carefully at the category for personnel.

Educational leaders spent a great deal on personnel. They used seventy percent of their funds to pay the salaries and benefits of teachers, clerks, technology specialists, accountants, medical consultants, cooks, maintenance laborers, electrical engineers, bus drivers, security guards, custodians, and groundskeepers (Giordano, 2012a).

The educational leaders examined and judged auxiliary workers. They noted that many of them were full-time workers.

The educational leaders concluded that they were spending too much on full-time auxiliary workers. Aware that they paid benefits only to their full-time employees, they detected a simple solution: they would replace them with part-timers.

Some educational leaders relied more heavily on part-time auxiliary workers to reduce spending. Others used a different strategy: they asked private vendors to supply low-cost auxiliary services. They then let the vendors decide how they would hire and pay workers (Giordano, 2012a).

Although educational leaders were concerned about the money that they spent on auxiliary workers, they were more concerned about that which they spent on teachers. They realized that they could save a great deal if they were to restrict the salaries of their teachers.

The educational leaders worried about plans to restrict teachers' salaries. They explained that these plans had risks as well as opportunities. They were particularly worried that they might cause strikes. Some of them restricted teachers' salaries anyway; others looked for another budgetary category in which to restrict spending.

Closing Schools

Educational leaders concluded that they could save money if they cut spending on facilities. In fact, they could save substantial amounts if they shut down entire buildings. Nonetheless, they fretted about how parents, school workers, neighborhood homeowners, and local business owners would respond to the closings (Hurdle, 2012).

When educational leaders were ready to cut spending on facilities, they did not want to be accused of being biased or capricious. They were impressed with the way in which businesspeople and sports leaders had used analytics to deflect these accusations. They decided to highlight their own reliance on analytics.

New York

Michael Bloomberg became the mayor of New York City in 2002. He appointed Joel Klein as his schools chancellor. The two men conceived a bold plan to improve local education. They made school closings a key component of that plan.

The mayor and chancellor resolved to close schools. However, they anticipated that parents would have questions. They knew the parents would badger them for the names of any schools that they had targeted for closing.

The mayor and chancellor hesitated to offer information about the schools that they would close. They were cautious because many of these schools were in minority neighborhoods. They instead offered in-

DOES ANALYTICS BELONG IN SCHOOLS?

formation about the manner in which they were making their decisions (Banchero & Porter, 2013b).

The mayor and chancellor assured constituents that they were making analytics-driven decisions. They explained that they were basing their decisions on the scores that students earned on standardized tests. They guaranteed that they would not close schools with high scores; they would not give this guarantee for schools with low scores.

The mayor and chancellor predicted that the school closing would have a major benefit: they would increase test scores of New York City's students. They asked for parental support.

Some parents conceded that the school closings might increase test scores. However, they worried that this increase would be offset by the damage to students, teachers, and entire neighborhoods. They were not comforted when they were assured that charter schools might be available in neighborhoods where public schools closed (Hurdle, 2012).

Philadelphia

School leaders in New York City began to shutter buildings. Ninety miles away, leaders in Philadelphia were getting ready to shutter some of the buildings in their own community.

The Philadelphians announced that they would close more than twenty schools in 2013. When they were asked for the names of the schools, they answered that they would use analytics to make this decision.

The Philadelphians stated that they were using a different analytics formula than the New Yorkers had employed. Instead of singling out the schools with low test scores, they were singling out those with inordinately high operating costs. They made it clear that their goal was to lower spending (Banchero & Maher, 2013; Hurdle, 2012; "Mayor's Education," 2013).

Chicago

Rahm Emanuel won Chicago's 2011 mayoral election. He immediately appointed new school board members. He directed them to focus on pressing problems.

Emanuel told the board members that Chicago's problems were related to its teachers, who were paid well but who underperformed. He directed board members to place financial restraints on teachers.

The board members came up with a plan to limit spending on teachers' salaries and benefits. They insisted that they used analytics to develop it.

The board members intended to implement their plan in 2012. They reckoned that it would upset teachers; they predicted that it even might prod them into a strike. They were correct: they did cause a teachers' strike.

The board members were eager to learn how the city's journalists would respond to the teachers' strike. They wondered which side they would support.

The board members were disappointed when they learned that most journalists sided with the teachers. They assumed that the journalists were influencing parents, who also sided with the teachers.

The board members had pledged to make no concessions to the striking teachers. However, they soon realized that the teachers were too formidable. After just a week, they capitulated to them (Giordano, 2014).

The school board members were despondent after the strike. They acknowledged that they had failed to reduce spending on teachers' salaries. However, they detected another opportunity to reduce spending.

The board members explained that they would close school buildings and reassign the students to new schools. They realized that they would have to close many schools and reassign numerous students in order to save a substantial amount.

The board members decided to close the schools of thirty thousand students. They calculated that they would reassign ten percent of their city's elementary-school pupils.

The board members were under pressure to disclose specific schools that they would close. Worried that they would be accused of using politics to make their decisions, they stated that they had used analytics.

The board members insisted that they had relied on analytics to identify schools with low enrollments, low test scores, and low funding. They eventually released their names.

When teachers and parents learned about the schools that would close, they were disgruntled. They complained about the enormous disruption associated with the closures.

The board members acknowledged that their plan would disrupt students and teachers. However, they argued that it also would save a significant amount of money. They predicted that it would save millions of dollars annually (Ahmed-Ullah & Secter, 2013; Banchero & Porter, 2013b; Davey, 2013).

Skeptics

Big-city mayors and school boards resolved to close educational facilities. They pledged that they would make bias-free decisions; they explained that they would rely on analytics.

Not all constituents had confidence in the mayors and school boards. Journalists suspected that mayors and school boards had mixed politics with analytics. Those in Chicago detected an explicit political objective: the mayor and school board wished to punish the teachers for their recent strike ("Rahm's Latest," 2013).

Parents were unhappy when the schools in their vicinity closed. They were not impressed when they were told that an analytics formula justified the closings. They were sure that the formula had not considered all of the academic risks that the closings entailed.

Parents also were concerned about the nonacademic risks of school closings. For example, they noted that some children were forced to attend schools within the territories of hostile urban gangs. They criticized the mayor and the school board for failing to discern this peril ("Chicago Kids," 2013).

EXAMINING ANALYTICS-BASED ANSWERS

Sports managers and business leaders depicted analytics as a bias-free type of decision making. They inspired persons to apply it to education.

Activity 2.1

The manager of the Oakland Athletics used analytics during losing streaks. How did groups respond?

Table 2.1 identifies two local groups: journalists and fans.

Complete the table by indicating the ways in which the groups responded to the manager. You can use symbols.

Use the symbol – if the groups exhibited low confidence in him. Use the symbol ± for moderate confidence and the symbol + for high confidence. As a final step, explain the bases for the symbols that you selected.

You can rely on the information in this chapter, additional information, or the information cited in the references. If you are reading this chapter with colleagues, you can confer with them.

Table 2.1. A Baseball Manager Uses Analytics during Losing Streaks

Groups	Response*	Explanation
Journalists		
Fans		

*– Low
± Moderate
+ High

Activity 2.2

The manager of the Oakland Athletics used analytics during winning streaks. How did groups respond?

Table 2.2 identifies two local groups: journalists and fans.

Complete the table by indicating the ways in which the groups responded to the manager. You can use symbols.

Use the symbol – if the groups exhibited low confidence in him. Use the symbol ± for moderate confidence and the symbol + for high confidence. As a final step, explain the bases for the symbols that you selected.

Table 2.2. A Baseball Manager Uses Analytics during Winning Streaks

Groups	Response*	Explanation
Journalists		
Fans		

*– Low
± Moderate
+ High

Activity 2.3

The members of Chicago's school board used analytics to restrict teachers' salaries. How did groups respond?

Table 2.3 identifies two local groups: journalists and parents.

Complete the table by indicating the ways in which the groups responded to the board members. You can use symbols.

Use the symbol – if the groups exhibited low confidence in them. Use the symbol ± for moderate confidence and the symbol + for high confidence. As a final step, explain the bases for the symbols that you selected.

Table 2.3. The Chicago School Board Uses Analytics to Restrict Teachers' Salaries

Groups	Response*	Explanation
Journalists		
Parents		

*– Low
± Moderate
+ High

Activity 2.4

The members of Chicago's school board used analytics to close schools. How did groups respond?

Table 2.4 identifies two local groups: journalists and parents.

Complete the table by indicating the ways in which the groups responded to the board members. You can use symbols.

Use the symbol − if the groups exhibited low confidence in them. Use the symbol ± for moderate confidence and the symbol + for high confidence. As a final step, explain the bases for the symbols that you selected.

Table 2.4. The Chicago School Board Uses Analytics to Close Schools

Groups	Response*	Explanation
Journalists		
Parents		

*− Low
± Moderate
+ High

SUMMARY

Sports managers and business leaders claimed that analytics enabled them to make bias-free decisions. School administrators made the same boast. However, all of these groups were challenged by skeptics.

3

DOES FOR-PROFIT IDEOLOGY MAKE SENSE IN PUBLIC EDUCATION?

[Corporations] can rescue schools and turn a profit.

—David Bennett, 1992

[The school] was a strange hybrid . . . publicly funded . . . but . . . for-profit.

—William Symonds, Ann Palmer, Dave Lindorff, & Jessica McCann, 2000

Eighty percent of Michigan charter schools are for-profits.

—Erik Kain, 2011

Public education has been a tough market for the private [for-profit] firms [to enter].

—Stephanie Simon, 2012

Are [for-profit] schools pocketing a large profit while cutting corners for students?

—Patrick O'Donnell, 2012

For-profit companies shouldn't be "getting paid" . . . when [we] parents . . . buy copy paper [for the schools].

—Patricia Johnson, quoted by Carr & Gilbertson, 2013

Trying to make profit off the education crisis is totally not cool.

—Mahala Papadopoulos, student, quoted by Piette, 2013

Teaching is not a business.

—David Kirpaug, 2014

*E*ntrepreneurs embraced capitalist ideology. They used it to justify a wide range of investments, including for-profit schools.

ENTREPRENEURIAL PATENT LITIGATION

Hundreds of thousands of people receive patents annually. They use them to gain legal protection for machines, designs, industrial procedures, plants, and composite materials.

People have another reason to get patents: they hope to generate income from them. They are disappointed when they do not.

Entrepreneurs realize that most patent owners receive no income from their intellectual properties. They offer to purchase them for modest prices. They are excited when the disillusioned owners accept their offers.

Enthusiasts

The entrepreneurs located business owners who might be using the patents that they had acquired. They demanded royalties from them. They threatened to sue if they did not pay.

Business owners were furious at the entrepreneurs. They depicted them as scavengers who extracted money without providing any service in exchange.

The entrepreneurs stated that they did provide a genuine business service; but they provided it to patent owners. They explained that they gave the patent owners the only money that they ever would receive for their intellectual property.

The entrepreneurs preferred to think of themselves as capitalists within an emerging field: patent litigation. Although they acknowledged that they made huge profits, they pointed out that they also took huge risks. They judged that their profits and risks were proportional to those of other businesspeople, including bankers, financiers, and real estate speculators (Fuchs, 2013).

The entrepreneurs were able to rationalize their actions. Nonetheless, they still were worried. They feared reprisals from the firms that they had sued. They needed allies to protect them.

The entrepreneurs asked lawyers to become allies. They were pleased when they were joined by the lawyers who had represented them in suits; they were even more pleased when they were joined by the lawyers who had represented the firms that they had sued (Kieff & Paredes, 2012; Rosenberg, 2013).

The patent entrepreneurs tried to attract journalists as allies. They realized that the journalists were important because of their influence. They hoped that journalists would persuade the public to value current patent laws; they hoped that journalists would persuade politicians to maintain those laws (Wyatt, 2013).

Skeptics

Business leaders were upset about the patent suits. Even when they were sure that they were frivolous, they had to pay enormous amounts for legal defense.

Business leaders had another reason to be upset. They realized that even frivolous patent suits disposed investors against their businesses. For this reason, many of them were eager to settle patent disagreements out of court (Matsuura, 2008).

The entrepreneurs also were eager to settle. However, they sometimes demanded millions of dollars. They pointed out that their settlement prices, even though they were high, were less than the prices for litigating disputes (Curtis, 2012).

The business leaders were upset about the high costs of fighting lawsuits; they were just as upset about the high costs of settling them. They realized that they needed allies. They took the same approach as their adversaries: they asked journalists to help them attract allies (Wyatt, 2013).

Journalists were willing to take the side of the business leaders. However, they realized that the legal issues could be difficult to grasp. They looked for a rhetorical tool that would make those issues accessible to the general public. They decided to employ a figure of speech: they would compare the patent entrepreneurs to commercial fisherpersons.

The journalists explained that commercial fisherpersons used enormous nylon nets to troll indiscriminately for oceanic creatures. They compared them to patent entrepreneurs, who formed nets from obscure patents and then trolled for financial prey (Fawcett, 2013).

Business leaders liked the metaphor; they noted that the journalists were able to attract some sympathizers. Nonetheless, they were not completely satisfied. They told the journalists that they primarily were arousing sympathy from fellow industrialists; they had hoped that they would arouse it from politicians (Feldman, 2012).

The business leaders wanted politicians to speak out against patent trolling. They were excited when President Obama decried the practice. They were even more excited when congressional leaders pledged to change the laws on which the practice depended (Hiltzik, 2013; Schumer, 2013).

ENTREPRENEURIAL SCHOOLS

Entrepreneurs looked for novel ways to make money. Some detected opportunities in public education.

Entrepreneurs had made money for decades through for-profit colleges and universities. They realized that they could make additional money through for-profit high schools, middle schools, elementary schools, and kindergartens.

Entrepreneurs began to establish K–12 schools during the late 1980s. However, they attracted scant students. At the end of the twentieth century, they were educating less than one-hundred thousand students across the entire nation. As a result, they generated little income (Bennett, 1992; Symonds, Palmer, Lindorff, & McCann, 2000).

The entrepreneurs persistently set up more and more K–12 schools. They convinced investors that these schools could grow large and become lucrative. One firm eventually employed fourteen thousand people and generated one-half-billion dollars in annual income (EdisonLearning, 2013).

Enthusiasts

The educational entrepreneurs created revenue; they also created controversy. They were pleased with the revenue; they were not pleased with the controversy.

The entrepreneurs realized that controversy and revenue were connected. They stirred up controversy because of the manner in which they treated revenue. They used a portion of the revenue to operate their schools; they sequestered the rest for profits.

The entrepreneurs did not worry about the way that profit-taking was viewed by corporate investors. They assumed that the investors approved of it.

The entrepreneurs did not worry about the way that profit-taking was viewed by the clients. They assumed that clients cared only about the prices of the services that the entrepreneurs provided to them.

Although the entrepreneurs did not have concerns about the way that some groups viewed profit-taking, they did have concerns about others. They were extremely concerned about parents. They realized that parents might not send their children to schools that compromised educational quality because of profit-taking.

The entrepreneurs assured parents that profit-taking was not deleterious. They maintained that it did not prevent them from hiring competent instructors or administrators. They added that it did not prevent them from securing adequate facilities, equipment, or technology.

The entrepreneurs contended that they could make profits from their schools because they had revenue left after they had taken care of personnel, facilities, equipment, and technology. They attributed the surplus revenue to cost-saving steps (Giordano, 2012a).

The entrepreneurs identified some of their cost-saving steps: they paid teachers low salaries, gave them minimal benefits, and offered them short-term employment contracts. They insisted that these steps affected instruction's cost but not its quality (Roth, 2012).

The entrepreneurs used test scores to validate the quality of the instruction at their schools. They pointed out that the scores at their schools were higher than those at traditional public schools. They added that high scores were evident even when schools were situated in neighborhoods where lower scores were prevalent (Banchero & Maher, 2013a; Snell, 2012).

The entrepreneurs waited to see how groups were responding to their assurances about quality. They were relieved when many parents agreed with them. However, they also wished to find out how politicians and business leaders were responding.

The entrepreneurs realized that politicians were indispensable because they determined whether for-profit schools were eligible for public educational funds. They hoped that politicians would be supportive (Davey, 2013; "Mayor's Education," 2013; Young, 2012).

The entrepreneurs hoped that business leaders would also support for-profit schools. They were optimistic because these leaders had faced problems similar to those that the educational entrepreneurs were confronting.

The business leaders had tried to reduce workforce expenses without affecting the quality of products and services. They had restrained salaries, reduced benefits, eliminated job security, and resisted unionization. They applauded the education entrepreneurs who copied them (Giordano, 2012b).

The business leaders even had a philosophical reason to support the educational entrepreneurs. They explained that competition, which was a critical element of capitalism, was absent from the public schools. They predicted that the competition from entrepreneurs would provide an energizing jolt (Picciano & Spring, 2013).

Skeptics

The K–12 entrepreneurs had supportive teachers. As one might expect, they had support from many of the teachers to whom they provided jobs.

Although some of the teachers at for-profit schools had confidence in their employers, others were skeptical. The skeptics were upset because their employers offered noncompetitive salaries, few benefits, and negligible job security.

Teachers at the for-profit schools had another reason for being skeptical. They questioned the streamlined, task-oriented, accountability-based procedures at their schools. They conceded that these procedures might be optimal for making profits; they doubted whether they were optimal for instructing students (Giordano, 2012b).

As for the teachers at traditional public schools, most of them were skeptical of the for-profit educational entrepreneurs. They predicted that the entrepreneurs would have a disastrous impact on traditional public schools. They noted that the entrepreneurs already had forced many of the traditional public schools to close (Banchero & Maher, 2013; Hurdle, 2013).

ENTREPRENEURIAL ONLINE SCHOOLS

Educational entrepreneurs were ready to instruct students. Nonetheless, they first had to attract them.

The entrepreneurs knew that they could attract students with first-rate teachers and facilities. However, they had to keep a portion of their budgets for profits. As a result, they had to limit the funds that they spent on teachers and facilities.

The entrepreneurs looked for less costly ways to lure students. They judged that flexible courses could be ideal. They originally offered flexible courses at brick-and-mortar schools. However, they realized that they could save more money if they offered them over the Internet. They hoped that clients would be impressed.

Parents were impressed by flexible online courses. They noted that the courses could be individualized to accommodate children's schedules and needs.

State legislators also were impressed by the online courses. They admired them because they were popular with parents; they also admired them because they were cheap. They were eager to promote them.

Legislators in Florida searched for a special way to promote online courses during the 1990s. They decided to establish the Florida Virtual School. They funded this statewide cyberschool as if it were an independent school district: they adjusted its revenue on the basis of the number of students that it served (Girdner, 2012).

Many students took courses from the Florida Virtual School. Even students who were enrolled in face-to-face courses took online courses as well.

The Florida Virtual School originally served only high-school students. However, it later offered courses to students in middle school, elementary school, and even kindergarten.

Some school districts organized their own virtual schools. They discovered that they could run them at little expense if they collaborated with the Florida Virtual School (Duval County Public Schools, 2010).

Enthusiasts

Florida's legislators expected their innovative and inexpensive cyberschool to benefit students. They also expected it to benefit school administrators.

The legislators required that all school administrators make online courses available to their students. However, the legislators hoped that the administrators would genuinely cherish the courses. They must have been pleased when the administrators in one district rhapsodized that the online courses had transformed students' learning into an "individualized adventure" (Duval County Public Schools, 2010).

Florida legislators needed allies to promote their new cyberschool. They already had taken steps to conscript school administrators. However, they wished to attract parents as well.

Many parents were enthusiastic about the cyberschool. Those who were homeschooling their children had been buying online courses from commercial vendors; they realized that the virtual school would supply its courses free.

Some parents viewed the cyberschool as an alternative route to graduation. They were grateful that it gave their children opportunities to retake those face-to-face courses that they had failed (Giordano, 2012b; "Thinking About," 2013; Thompson, 2013).

Some parents valued the cyberschool because it provided individualized instruction to their children. They were happy that children could progress through courses at their own pace and complete only those units with which they had struggled during face-to-face classes.

Florida legislators were pleased that parents supported their new cyberschool. However, they were not completely satisfied. They hoped that business leaders would support it as well.

The business leaders were supportive. They commended the cyberschool for cost-saving measures such as the hiring of nonunionized teachers and noncertified instructor aides.

The business leaders became even more excited about the Florida Virtual School after it established a partnership with a for-profit firm. They encouraged it to form partnerships with other private-sector firms ("Company Overview," 2013; McGrory, 2013).

Skeptics

Not all persons were enthusiastic about the Florida Virtual School. Skeptics faulted it for draining critical resources from traditional public schools.

Some parents were skeptical of the school's partnership with a for-profit firm. They were distressed by the amount of revenue sequestered for advertising and profit-taking. They preferred that this revenue go to instruction (Giordano, 2012a; Lopez, 2013).

Some of the teachers who worked in traditional public schools viewed the cyberschool as their competitor. They complained that they were at a disadvantage because the cyberschool received a more generous type of funding ("Florida Virtual School Reviews," 2013).

The teachers in traditional schools had questions about the instructors at the cyberschool. They noted that some of the instructors did not have appropriate teaching certificates (Giordano, 2012b; O'Connor, 2012).

The teachers in traditional schools had questions about how students were assessed at the cyberschool. For example, they wondered how students were evaluated in online physical education courses (Gonzalez, 2012).

Even some of the teachers at the cyberschool had questions about their employer's practices. They questioned whether salaries were equitable, benefits reasonable, job security adequate, due process available, and grading policies ethical ("Florida Virtual School Employer," 2013; "Florida Virtual School Reviews," 2013; O'Connor, 2012).

EXAMINING IDEOLOGICAL QUESTIONS

Entrepreneurs valued capitalist ideology. Some of them used it to rationalize patent litigation; some used it to rationalize for-profit education. They attracted the attention of sympathizers and skeptics.

Activity 3.1

Entrepreneurs trolled for potential patent violators, demanded royalties from them, and threatened to sue if they did not pay. How did groups respond to them?

Table 3.1 identifies two groups: politicians and business leaders.

Complete the table by indicating the ways in which the groups responded to the entrepreneurs. You can use symbols.

Use the symbol – if the groups exhibited low confidence in the entrepreneurs. Use the symbol ± for moderate confidence and the symbol + for high confidence. As a final step, explain the bases for the symbols that you selected.

You can rely on the information in this chapter, additional information, or the information cited in the references. If you are reading this chapter with colleagues, you can confer with them.

Table 3.1. Entrepreneurs Engage in Patent Trolling

Groups	Response*	Explanation
Politicians		
Business Leaders		

*– Low
± Moderate
+ High

Activity 3.2

Entrepreneurs established for-profit schools. How did groups respond?

Table 3.2 identifies two groups: politicians and business leaders.

Complete the table by indicating the ways in which the groups responded to the entrepreneurs. You can use symbols.

Use the symbol – if the groups exhibited low confidence in the entrepreneurs. Use the symbol ± for moderate confidence and the symbol + for high confidence. As a final step, explain the bases for the symbols that you selected.

Table 3.2. Entrepreneurs Establish For-Profit Schools

Groups	Response*	Explanation
Politicians		
Business Leaders		

*– Low
± Moderate
+ High

DOES FOR-PROFIT IDEOLOGY MAKE SENSE IN PUBLIC EDUCATION? 39

Activity 3.3

Entrepreneurs collaborated with the Florida Virtual School. How did groups respond?

Table 3.3 identifies two groups: politicians and business leaders.

Complete the table by indicating the ways in which the groups responded to the entrepreneurs. You can use symbols.

Use the symbol – if the groups exhibited low confidence in the entrepreneurs. Use the symbol ± for moderate confidence and the symbol + for high confidence. As a final step, explain the bases for the symbols that you selected.

Table 3.3. Entrepreneurs Collaborate with the Florida Virtual School

Groups	Response*	Explanation
Politicians		
Business Leaders		

*– Low
± Moderate
+ High

SUMMARY

Entrepreneurs extolled capitalist ideology. Some of them made it the basis for patent litigation; others made it the basis of for-profit education.

4

CAN SCHOOL LEADERS GET SOME THINGS FOR NOTHING?

Focus on [school] customer service . . . will . . . result in improved academic achievement.

—Kelly Middleton & Elizabeth Petitt, 2007

The customer service approach . . . starts with . . . reminding all [school] staff members to greet visitors.

—Ellen Delisio, 2009

[Our school] district has made a commitment to . . . customer service.

—Austin Independent School District, 2011

Schools must find ways to become more customer service "savvy."

—Karen Kleinz, 2013

There is so much you can tell about a school by talking to the front desk.

—Boldrin Gwinn, quoted by Rayworth, 2014

Business leaders prized customer-relations strategies because they were inexpensive yet effective. They made an impression on school administrators.

AIRLINE EXECUTIVES

Airline executives wished to maximize profits. They realized that they could achieve this goal only if their passengers were satisfied. They resolved to monitor passenger attitudes toward facilities, equipment, amenities, technology, and personnel.

The executives assumed that passenger satisfaction could determine whether their corporations prospered. For this reason, they were especially attentive to it when profits were low.

The executives at Delta learned that they might have a problem with their passengers in 2009. They were advised that many customers were leaving unflattering comments on travel websites (Liebman, 2012).

The executives were surprised. After all, they were earning extremely high profits during this period. They wondered whether a nonrepresentative group of travelers might have posted negative comments. They therefore combed through industry-wide surveys. They were distressed when they discovered that all of the surveys contained negative comments about Delta ("Delta One of Top," 2009; McWilliams, 2011).

Passengers clearly were unhappy with Delta. They had ranked it as the worst airline in the industry. They fired withering broadsides at its employees, whom they characterized as discourteous, unprofessional, uncommunicative, and unpunctual. They eventually got the attention of Delta's executives.

The executives initiated a corporation-wide campaign. They enjoined their managers to model customer-relations strategies. They required all of their workers to read customer-relations information; they required many of them to attend intensive workshops (McCartney, 2011).

The executives wondered whether their campaign was having an impact on passengers. They examined websites for recent postings. They were relieved when they found many positive comments.

The executives looked for additional evidence that their campaign was having an impact. They examined how Delta was scoring on industry-wide surveys of customer satisfaction. They cheered as it moved out of last place, rose in the rankings, and then ascended to first place (Reed, 2013).

The executives were asked how they had engineered such a remarkable turnaround. They answered that some of their employees always had exhibited exemplary customer-relations skills. However, they acknowledged that others had benefited from training.

Enthusiasts

Business leaders paid attention to the customer-relations campaign at Delta. They concluded that it had been a huge success. They noted that it persuaded passengers to write positive testimonials about the carrier and assign high scores to it on surveys.

Business leaders praised Delta's campaign for another reason: it had cost very little to implement. They noted that it had relied on inexpensive workshops, bulletins, and on-the-job coaching (Bacal, 2011; Kamin, 2006).

Skeptics

People did not question that Delta's customer-relations campaign had been successful. Nonetheless, some of them questioned the alleged reasons for its success.

The skeptics doubted that Delta ever had a significant problem. They judged that many of the customers' complaints originated with the airports upon which Delta relied rather than the airline itself.

The skeptics explained that Delta used the Atlanta airport as its primary hub. They noted that this facility had been rated by flyers as the worst in the nation. They reasoned that Delta's customer-relations campaign had convinced passengers that they should not blame the carrier for an airport's problems.

The skeptics noted that Delta generated more than thirty billion dollars annually; they concluded that it was a successful and admired corporation. They judged that it had benefited from customer-relations "charm schools" precisely because it was facing easy-to-handle problems. They noted that airlines with hard-to-handle problems had not benefited from comparable campaigns ("Delta Tops," 2013; Kenney, 2011; McCartney, 2011).

PRINCIPALS

Parents set high goals for principals. They expected them to hire first-rate teachers, carefully supervise auxiliary staffs, maintain physical facilities, arrange reliable transportation, safeguard students, update textbooks, secure technology, and confirm that students were learning.

Principals developed comprehensive administrative plans. They tried to make sure that their plans encompassed all of the goals that the parents had set. Nonetheless, they realized that they did not have the resources to pursue all of the goals with equal energy.

The principals noted that some goals required costly strategies while others required less costly strategies. Although they were able to adopt some expensive strategies, they tried to complement them with ones that were less expensive.

The principals looked to business leaders for examples of inexpensive strategies. They were fascinated by customer-relations strategies.

One principal learned about customer-relations strategies while he was staying at an upscale hotel. He witnessed the hotel manager use them during a casual interaction.

The principal asked the manager to show him the kitchen. The manager responded that he would love to honor this request. Nonetheless, he could not comply because the principal was not wearing an outfit that was appropriate for entering the kitchen.

The principal was fully aware that the manager had turned him down. He insisted that he still felt fine because of the manner in which the manager communicated the denial.

The principal had formed an important insight: one should avoid saying "no" to customers. He had learned how to artfully convey a denial. He resolved to use this cost-free strategy when he was dealing with parents at school ("In Georgia," 2013).

Enthusiasts

Principals were enthusiastic about customer-relations strategies. They viewed them as inexpensive but effective ways to improve educational services.

Some principals personally used customer-relations strategies to deal with parents and members of the public. Others required their teachers and auxiliary workers to use them.

Enthusiasts detected an impact from customer-relations strategies. They inspired their fellow administrators to copy them.

When principals wished to train their staffs about customer relations, some of them distributed information from the National School Public Relations Association. Others personally provided training. Still others hired specialists to provide training (Austin Independent School District, 2011; DeLapp, 2007; National School Public Relations Association, 2013).

Skeptics

Principals understood that parents were irked by school problems. They judged that some of the problems with which they dealt were manageable. For example, they had to deal with tardy school transportation, long lunch lines, inadequate extracurricular activities, unpopular teachers, worn textbooks, and dysfunctional technology.

When principals used customer-relations strategies to deal with manageable problems, they were pleased with the results. They conceded that the strategies did not actually eliminate the problems. Nonetheless, they valued the strategies because they helped the parents realize that the problems were not dire. They also valued them because they directed parents' attention to positive features of their schools.

Principals sometimes faced truly daunting problems. They had to deal with unsafe facilities, crime, poverty, disease, substance addiction, racism, teenage pregnancy, child abuse, bullying, and weapons on school campuses.

The principals who faced hard-to-manage problems were skeptical of customer-relations strategies. They judged that the strategies did not alleviate the problems; they added that they did not alter the perspectives from which parents viewed the problems (Giordano, 2012a, 2012b; Kowalski, 2000; Middleton & Petitt, 2007; Moore, 2009).

SUPERINTENDENTS

Most superintendents had tight budgets. They dreaded potential reductions to them.

The superintendent in Jacksonville, Florida, was alarmed about reductions to his budget. He claimed that he already had lost forty-nine million dollars to local charter schools (Brooks, 2013b).

The superintendent needed strategies to discourage parents from pulling children out of his schools and sending them to charter schools instead. He decided to use customer-relations strategies. He directed his principals, teachers, professional staff members, and auxiliary workers to use them as well (Brooks, 2013b).

The superintendent had a topic to which he was ready to apply customer-relations strategies. However, he soon realized that the school board was more interested in other topics.

When the school board's members had appointed the superintendent, they advised him to deal with serious academic issues. As just one example, he would be responsible for the lowest performing high school in the state (Giordano, 2012a; Stepzinski, 2012).

The school board members also wanted the superintendent to deal with troublesome nonacademic issues. They noted that one of these issues had been smoldering for decades.

In 1959, school board members had to select a name for a new high school. They wanted to honor an extremely distinguished individual. They selected Nathan Bedford Forrest, who had been a Civil War general and the leader of the Ku Klux Klan.

Nathan Bedford Forrest High School was set up as a segregated school: it was available only to white students. However, it went through changes during the Civil Rights Era. It was desegregated and relocated to a different neighborhood.

Although the school went through changes, it continued to stir up residents. It upset some of them because of its name—Nathan Bedford Forrest High School.

One resident posted an online petition in 2013. He asked individuals to sign it if they preferred that the school be named for someone who had not been a leader of a racist organization. He must have been surprised by the response: tens of thousands of persons signed the petition (Brooks, 2013a).

Journalists at national tabloids publicized the name-change petition. Referring to the school as "KKK High School," they clearly signaled their disdain for its name (Hastings, 2013; "Petition Targets," 2013; Strauss, 2013b).

The superintendent was asked whether he preferred the school's current name or a new one. He realized that those residents who supported the name and those who opposed it were waiting for his response. He recognized that journalists also were waiting.

The superintendent used customer-relations skills when he answered the question. He replied that he might be ready to recommend a name change. However, he immediately added that he would recommend it only if it were supported by groups with "organic" links to the community (Brooks, 2013a).

Enthusiasts

Jacksonville residents pondered the superintendent's response. Those who opposed the name change were optimistic. They assumed that the superintendent was critical of the outsiders who were raising a commotion.

Those Jacksonville residents who opposed the name change admired Nathan Bedford Forrest. They reasoned that he had lived during a distinct historical era and should be judged by the social and cultural standards of that era. They concluded that he deserved the honor of a school with his name.

The journalists at Jacksonville's local newspaper opposed the name change. They published a lead editorial in which they urged persons in the community to disregard advice from outsiders. They directed them to focus on the school's academic performance rather than its name.

The local journalists were pleased by the way that the superintendent had answered the name-change question. They assumed that he was distancing himself from outside pressure groups ("Focus on the Real Issue," 2013).

Skeptics

Some Jacksonville residents wanted the board to change the school's name. However, they realized that the board would not act without the endorsement of the superintendent. They had tried but failed to get endorsements from former superintendents. They were skeptical of getting one from the current superintendent because of his nuanced answer to the name-change question.

The local journalists had opposed the name-change petition. Nonetheless, they kept their eyes on the number of persons who were signing it. They were in disbelief when that number increased to more than one hundred and fifty thousand persons.

The local journalists realized that Jacksonville's business leaders were upset about the way that their community was being portrayed in national media. They were being pressured by the businesspeople to take a different position on the name change. They began to have second thoughts.

The local journalists published a new editorial. They announced that they had reversed their stance on the high school's name. They explained that its name had been "poisoned" and no longer could be retained.

The local journalists also reversed their prediction about the superintendent. They predicted that he would endorse the name change because he had discovered that the group spearheading it did have an "organic" link to the community ("It's Time," 2013).

EXAMINING CUSTOMER-RELATIONS STRATEGIES

Business leaders claimed that customer-relations strategies were inexpensive yet effective. They made an impression on school leaders.

Activity 4.1

The executives at Delta Airlines recommended that employees use customer-relations strategies to deal with disconsolate passengers. How did groups respond?

Table 4.1 identifies two groups: Delta passengers and the executives at other airlines.

CAN SCHOOL LEADERS GET SOME THINGS FOR NOTHING? 49

Complete the table by indicating the ways in which the groups responded to the executives. You can use symbols.

Use the symbol – if the groups exhibited low confidence in them. Use the symbol ± for moderate confidence and the symbol + for high confidence. As a final step, explain the bases for the symbols that you selected.

You can rely on the information in this chapter, additional information, or the information cited in the references. If you are reading this chapter with colleagues, you can confer with them.

Table 4.1. Delta Uses Customer Relations

Groups	Response*	Explanation
Passengers		
Executives		

*– Low
± Moderate
+ High

Activity 4.2

Principals used customer-relations strategies to deal with disconsolate parents. How did groups respond?

Table 4.2 identifies two groups: parents and principals at other schools.

Complete the table by indicating the ways in which the groups responded to the principals. You can use symbols.

Use the symbol – if the groups exhibited low confidence in them. Use the symbol ± for moderate confidence and the symbol + for high confidence. As a final step, explain the bases for the symbols that you selected.

Table 4.2. Principals Use Customer Relations

Groups	Response*	Explanation
Parents		
Principals		

*– Low
± Moderate
+ High

CAN SCHOOL LEADERS GET SOME THINGS FOR NOTHING?

Activity 4.3

A Florida superintendent used customer-relations strategies to deal with persons who were disconsolate about a school's name. How did groups respond?

Table 4.3 identifies two groups: parents and journalists.

Complete the table by indicating the ways in which the groups responded to the superintendent. You can use symbols.

Use the symbol – if the groups exhibited low confidence in him. Use the symbol ± for moderate confidence and the symbol + for high confidence. As a final step, explain the bases for the symbols that you selected.

Table 4.3. A Superintendent Uses Customer Relations

Groups	Response*	Explanation
Parents		
Journalists		

*– Low
± Moderate
+ High

SUMMARY

Business leaders claimed that customer-relations strategies were inexpensive yet effective. They made an impression on school administrators, who applied them to public education.

5

HOW ARE EDUCATIONAL QUESTIONS FRAMED?

[Framing] has to do with choosing the language to define a debate.

—Matt Bai, 2005

The debate is framed around the idea that our schools are failing.

—Bill Stamatis, 2009

The school-reform debate is in large part a matter of . . . framing.

—Jonathan Mahler, 2011

Why do the media nearly always frame education issues as the [teachers union] vs. the Mayor.

—New York City Public School Parents, 2013

[The mayor has been] framing the change [in teacher evaluation] as the culmination of his work.

—Lisa Fleisher, 2013

Logic matters little in a world where facts are twisted to fit narratives.

—Sabrina Tavernise, 2014

Businesspeople and politicians demonstrated the power of framing. They made an impression on educators.

BUSINESS

Lululemon began to market upscale yoga clothing during the 1990s. It quickly became a multibillion-dollar business.

Observers were impressed by Lululemon's growth. They asked executives at the firm to reveal their secret strategies.

The executives stated that that they did not have secret strategies; they used routine marketing procedures. They carefully framed products through pricing, inventory control, and store design. They then examined customer feedback to confirm that they had made the right decisions (Bhasin, 2013).

The executives at Lululemon stressed the importance of customer feedback. However, they did not obtain this information with the standard marketing tools; they eschewed online chats, telephone calls, written surveys, focus groups, and face-to-face interviews. They feared that the information collected through these procedures would be biased (Bradburn, Sudman, & Wansink, 2004).

The executives came up with an ingenious way to obtain customer feedback. They told their sales associates to take advantage of the worktables next to their shoppers' dressing stalls.

The sales associates gave the appearance of being fully occupied at the worktables: they labeled, folded, marked, and hung clothing. However, they also were listening to the remarks of the nearby shoppers (Mattioli, 2012).

Journalists eventually discovered that Lululemon was snooping on customers. They used the discovery to frame the retailer. They anticipated that their allegations would change the way that customers viewed Lululemon. However, they were mistaken (Clifford, 2013; Matthews, 2013; A. Smith, 2013).

Customers showed little interest in the information from the journalists. As a result, they were hardly influenced by their framing strategies. They were influenced to a much greater extent by the retailer's framing strategies.

POLITICS

Like businesspeople, politicians realized that framing was powerful. They applied it to speeches, advertisements, and website postings.

Partisans

Democrats hired media consultants to frame their information. Although they were pleased by the ways that the voters responded, they worried that some of the voters might be disconcerted. After all, framing had an effect on nationally important issues.

The Democrats were not worried about the ways that all voters viewed framing. They suspected that a large number of them could not even detect it. They anticipated that some of those who could detect it would view it as just another rhetorical tool (Huang, 2011).

The Democrats accurately anticipated the ways that voters would react to framing. However, they failed to anticipate the way that their political rivals would react.

Republicans criticized the Democrats. They thought that they had used framing to advance partisan goals rather than clarify issues. They made the same accusation against the Democrat-leaning journalists who used framing (Bozell, 2013; Goldberg, 2001; Ladd, 2012).

The Democrats denied the accusations about irresponsible framing; they claimed that the Republican politicians were guilty of this practice. They also made this claim about Republican-leaning journalists.

The Democrats were upset because Republicans employed framing. They may have been even more upset because the Republicans employed it in such a sophisticated manner (Bothmer, 2010; Johnson-Cartee, 2005; Mooney, 2010).

The Democrats decried framing not just within publications, but also within broadcasts. They gave examples from the radio broadcasts of Rush Limbaugh and the television broadcasts of FOX News. Even President Obama expressed his annoyance at these broadcasts ("Barack Obama Complains," 2009; "Obama: Republicans," 2013).

Special-Interest Groups

Special-interest groups were impressed when politicians used framing. They decided to copy them.

Right-to-life groups framed information in ways that would curtail abortions; their opponents framed information to expand opportunities. Anti-immigration groups framed information to reduce employment of illegal aliens; opponents framed it to increase opportunities. Some groups framed information to restrict federal defense spending; others framed it to enhance this spending (Burns, 2005; Entman, 2003).

Although special-interest groups admired the ways that politicians had used framing, they also admired the way that politicians accused opponents of irresponsible framing. They were impressed by the damage that politicians caused with these accusations. The special-interest groups made accusations of framing against their own opponents. They accused their opponents of recklessly framing information about topics such as race, religion, and economic justice (Graham, 2001; Kendall, 2005; Morey & Yaqin, 2011; Rhodes, 2007).

SCHOOL SAFETY

Parents of public-school children made requests for specialized or enhanced academic services. They made them for nonacademic services as well. They channeled the requests to school administrators.

The parents realized that the school administrators were deluged with requests. They therefore assigned priorities to them. They implored administrators to expedite those requests that they designated as high-priority.

Parents in Los Angeles were concerned about safety in their schools. Those with children in high-crime neighborhoods were extremely concerned. They requested that school administrators take extraordinary steps to protect their children. They made it clear that this request had high priority.

The school administrators hesitated to take special protective steps. They reasoned that the children already were well protected; they explained that they were protected by the hundreds of school police officers who regularly patrolled their buildings.

The parents were not satisfied. They worried that armed assailants could evade or overwhelm the officers. They became much more anxious in 2012: an assailant entered the Sandy Hook Elementary School in Connecticut and murdered twenty-six persons.

The school administrators recognized that the parents were unnerved by the tragedy in Connecticut. They assured them that they would take steps to prevent a tragedy in California. They equipped their police officers with high-powered, semiautomatic rifles; they gave them permission to use them in the schools (Flaccus, 2013).

The President

Parents across the nation were horrified by the events in Connecticut. They wondered whether similar events could transpire in their own communities. They posed this question to politicians.

President Obama had a response: he told the parents that their children were not safe. He explained that they were at risk because of the ease with which citizens could purchase guns. He called for additional restrictions on gun purchases (Steinhauer, 2013).

Journalists faithfully summarized the details of the president's proposal. However, they questioned whether it genuinely would increase school safety.

The journalists argued that the president's proposal would not protect children in many situations. They noted that it would not have prevented the Connecticut school assailant, who had used lawfully acquired weapons that he found in his own home.

Journalists questioned whether the president's proposal was legal. They noted that it might circumvent the constitutionally guaranteed right to carry arms (Rivkin & Grossman, 2013).

Journalists chided the president for failing to confer with mental-health professionals. They noted that these professionals believed that improved psychological services would promote school safety more effectively than gun regulations (Angulo, 2013; Goode, 2013).

Journalists noted that some parents were disappointed with the president for focusing exclusively on regulations for guns. They identified parents who wanted regulations for violent video games (Lichtblau, 2013).

Educators

Some persons believed that they could protect children by making guns less accessible. Others judged that they could protect them by making them more accessible.

The leaders of the National Rifle Association wanted to place more guns in the schools. However, they wanted to place them in the hands of police officers. They recommended that armed officers be stationed at every school.

Journalists noted that the NRA plan was popular; they added that it was extremely expensive. They feared that educators would have to take money from already lean instructional budgets to pay for it. They looked for less costly options (Banchero & Porter, 2013a; Stolberg, 2013).

The journalists highlighted inexpensive ways to get protective weapons into schools. They noted that many educators, who already had weapons and the permits to carry them, could not bring their weapons to school because of restrictive state laws. They described initiatives to change those laws (Eligon, 2013; Taylor, 2013).

The journalists stated that parents wanted principals and teachers to carry guns. However, they added that parents also wanted principals and teachers to complete training in marksmanship and gun safety. They looked for instances of this training (Bernat, 2012).

The legislators in some states authorized school administrators to provide marksmanship and gun-safety classes in their schools. Legislators must have been gratified when many of the administrators arranged these classes for their staffs (Foster, 2012; "Utah Teachers," 2012).

Teachers in Texas were authorized to bring handguns into classrooms. However, they first had to attend guns-in-schools training. They also had to obtain concealed-weapons permits and mental-health evaluations (Severson, 2013).

Like legislators, police officers gave advice about protecting schoolchildren. Some advised educators to bring guns to school, stand their ground, and confront intruders. Others counseled them to gather the children and flee (Johnson, 2013).

Insurance companies had reservations about educators bringing guns into the schools. Although they conceded that they could be effective, they predicted that guns in schools would cause accidental injuries and deaths. Some of them stated that they could provide insurance, but only for high premiums; others categorically refused to provide insurance (Yaccino, 2013).

Entrepreneurs

Administrators were wary of guns in schools. Some worried that they would fail to protect schoolchildren. Others worried that they could accidentally harm schoolchildren. Still others worried that they would make insurance premiums unaffordable.

Those school administrators who were wary of guns still wished to protect students. They tried to locate alternative safety measures. They turned to entrepreneurs for assistance.

The entrepreneurs were ready to help. They had products to prevent assailants from entering school buildings. As examples, they offered security cameras, metal detectors, electronic lockout doors, and rugged perimeter fences ("Schools Seek," 2012).

The entrepreneurs also had equipment to protect children after assailants entered schools. For example, they offered special antiballistic windows and whiteboards to protect children from stray bullets (Porter, 2014).

Some of the entrepreneurs marketed antiballistic items directly to the parents. For example, they sold bulletproof backpacks. They explained that these packs would shield children during attacks by armed intruders. They were pleased when journalists circulated details about their products (Connor, 2013).

EXAMINING FRAMED INFORMATION

Businesspeople demonstrated the power of framing. They made an impression on politicians and educators. All three of these groups framed information about school safety.

Activity 5.1

Lululemon executives used framing to prod sales of products. How did groups respond?

Table 5.1 identifies two groups: journalists and consumers.

Complete the table by indicating the ways in which the groups responded to the executives. You can use symbols.

Use the symbol – if the groups exhibited low interest. Use the symbol ± for moderate interest and the symbol + for high interest. As a final step, explain the bases for the symbols that you selected.

You can rely on the information in this chapter, additional information, or the information cited in the references. If you are reading this chapter with colleagues, you can confer with them.

Table 5.1. A Retailer Frames Products

Groups	Response*	Explanation
Journalists		
Consumers		

*– Low
± Moderate
+ High

Activity 5.2

Politicians used framing to prod changes to legislation and litigation. How did groups respond?

Table 5.2 identifies two groups: journalists and voters.

Complete the table by indicating the ways in which the groups responded to the politicians. You can use symbols.

Use the symbol – if the groups exhibited low interest. Use the symbol ± for moderate interest and the symbol + for high interest. As a final step, explain the bases for the symbols that you selected.

Table 5.2. Politicians Frame Legislation and Litigation

Groups	Response*	Explanation
Journalists		
Voters		

*– Low
± Moderate
+ High

Activity 5.3

President Obama used framing to prod changes to gun control laws. How did groups respond?

Table 5.3 identifies two groups: journalists and parents.

Complete the table by indicating the ways in which the groups responded to the president. You can use symbols.

Use the symbol – if the groups exhibited low interest. Use the symbol ± for moderate interest and the symbol + for high interest. As a final step, explain the bases for the symbols that you selected.

Table 5.3. A President Frames Gun Control Legislation

Groups	Response*	Explanation
Journalists		
Parents		

*– Low
± Moderate
+ High

Activity 5.4

Educators used framing to prod changes to school safety procedures. How did groups respond?

Table 5.4 identifies two groups: journalists and parents.

Complete the table by indicating the ways in which the groups responded to the educators. You can use symbols.

Use the symbol – if the groups exhibited low interest. Use the symbol ± for moderate interest and the symbol + for high interest. As a final step, explain the bases for the symbols that you selected.

Table 5.4. Educators Frame School Safety Procedures

Groups	Response*	Explanation
Journalists		
Parents		

*– Low
± Moderate
+ High

Activity 5.5

Entrepreneurs used framing to prod sales of safety-related school equipment. How did groups respond?

Table 5.5 identifies two groups: journalists and parents.

Complete the table by indicating the ways in which the groups responded to the entrepreneurs. You can use symbols.

Use the symbol – if the groups exhibited low interest. Use the symbol ± for moderate interest and the symbol + for high interest. As a final step, explain the bases for the symbols that you selected.

Table 5.5. Entrepreneurs Frame Safety-Related School Equipment

Groups	Response*	Explanation
Journalists		
Parents		

*– Low
± Moderate
+ High

SUMMARY

Businesspeople used framing to influence people's attitudes. They made an impression on politicians and educators.

6

DO CHARTER SCHOOLS IMPROVE PUBLIC EDUCATION?

Critics say that [charter schools] pull far too much money.

—Derek Kravitz, 2013

Less than 1% of federal education dollars go to [charter schools].

—"Will Obama's Budget," 2013

The Florida Department of Education [reported] . . . that charter school students outperform students at traditional schools.

—Scott Travis, 2013

More than 86 percent of the [Florida] charter schools do not serve a single child with a severe disability.

—"No Choice," 2013

[The] Florida Education Commissioner [resigned after he] . . . boosted a charter school's grade.

—John O'Connor, 2013

[Competition among charter schools is] like the "Hunger Games."

—Michael Mulgrew, quoted by Hernández, 2014

Obama has used his bully pulpit to champion charter schools.

—Jason Riley, 2014

People sometimes would not answer questions. They explained that they refused to answer any that came from partisan groups.

A MAINE COLLEGE

Bowdoin College is a small liberal arts institution in Maine. It attracted little notice for decades. However, it received a great deal of attention after a 2010 golf outing.

The president of Bowdoin College had been golfing with a philanthropist. As he moved about the course, he discussed his administrative philosophy.

The president stated that he had a responsibility to nurture socially progressive viewpoints among his students. He used this conviction to explain why he hired only those faculty members who shared his political views.

The philanthropist chastised the president for his monolithic hiring practices. He argued that he would help students more if he hired faculty members with ideologically diverse views.

The two men did not resolve their disagreement. However, the president was determined to have the last word on the matter. In a speech that he gave at his college's annual commencement ceremony, he recounted his golf-match remarks; he depicted his antagonist as an incorrigible bigot.

Posing Questions

The president assumed that he had made the final sally in the dispute about college hiring practices. However, he had underestimated his opponent.

The philanthropist learned of the remarks that the president had made to the commencement audience. He decided that he also wanted the chance to address a broad audience.

The philanthropist hired a scholar to investigate the intellectual culture at Bowdoin College. He directed him to present his results within a formal report.

The for-hire scholar examined the goals of the institution. He also examined the publications, speeches, and web postings of the faculty and administrators. He detailed his findings in a lengthy document.

The scholar acknowledged that Bowdoin's administrators and faculty had aspired to inculcate a broad, intellectual perspective among students. However, he judged that they had pursued this goal in such a doctrinaire manner that they had fostered a narrow and rigid perspective instead (Johnson & Thomas, 2013).

Ignoring Questions

The president of Bowdoin College was furious when he learned of the critical report. He insisted that it came from a scholar who had been hired to discredit him and his institution. He announced that he would ignore the allegations in it. He adjured colleagues at other colleges to do the same.

Many persons promised to follow the president's advice. Nonetheless, some did not take the pledge.

The members of an influential political institute announced that they had read the report, sympathized with it, and were going to "sponsor" it. They hoped to attract the attention of journalists. They were successful.

Journalists were fascinated by the Bowdoin report. They summarized its key points; they recounted the colorful incidents that had led to it. They pounced on the president and demanded additional details from him (Robinson, 2013; Russell, 2013).

Reactions

The president was upset by the inquisitive journalists. He also was upset by the scholar who had written the critical report, the philanthropist who had commissioned it, and the institute that had sponsored it.

The president stated that he would not answer any questions. He explained that he detected bias among the journalists, the philanthropist, the scholar, and the members of the sponsoring institute.

In spite of his bluster, the president was nervous. He was concerned that the critics might influence his key constituents. He worried that they would influence the parents of current students, the parents of potential students, and the college's donors.

The president was prescient about his constituents. They were influenced by the critics' questions. In fact, they began to repeat them.

The president realized that his constituents were not partisan groups. Nonetheless, he judged that their questions had been planted by partisan groups. He therefore refused to answer them.

FLORIDA CHARTER SCHOOLS

Florida legislators had approved charter schools during the late 1990s. They hoped that they would flourish. In fact, they took steps to ensure that they would flourish.

The legislators gave the charter schools generous financing. They provided them with funding comparable to that of traditional public schools.

The legislators excused charter schools from some regulations. They exempted them from onerous accountability measures to which the traditional schools had to adhere.

The legislators gave the charter schools special prerogatives. They allowed them to hire nonunionized teachers, appoint nontraditional school administrators, adopt novel curricula, experiment with innovative instruction, use distinctive learning materials, and employ atypical disciplinary procedures.

The legislators allowed charter schools to bypass the politicized and bureaucratic process through which the sites for new schools were designated; they allowed them to select their own sites. They also allowed them to select the neighborhoods from which they would draw students.

Posing Questions

Not all persons had confidence in Florida's charter schools. Unionized teachers did not conceal their skepticism.

The unionized teachers noted that the charter schools were attracting students from the population that the unionized teachers served. They calculated that the charter schools eventually were drawing one out of every seventeen students. They predicted that the charter schools would draw an even higher ratio. They asked their state legislators how the shifting enrollments would affect their own schools ("Everything You Need," 2013).

The unionized teachers noted that the charter schools were taking their funds as well as their students. They wanted to know the exact amounts. The teachers in one community were dazed when they were told that the charter schools had extracted tens of millions of dollars from their local, traditional education budget (Brooks, 2013b).

The unionized teachers noted that the personnel at the charter schools worked for lower wages. They wanted to know whether traditional public-school teachers would be pressured to limit salaries and benefits.

Unionized teachers had questions about the procedures through which charter schools assessed academic achievement. They asked whether state bureaucrats were monitoring charter-school procedures in the same manner that they did traditional schools. They were incensed when they learned that Florida's education commissioner had altered student-achievement data to create a more positive image of a charter school (Jordan, 2013; O'Connor, 2013).

Unionized teachers had questions about the salaries that the charter schools were paying to principals. They fumed when one school hired a principal for over three-hundred thousand dollars annually ("Florida's Shameful," 2012; Roth, 2012).

Unionized teachers wanted to know whether charter schools were enrolling students with disabilities. They worried that the charter schools might be avoiding students with disabilities to bolster test score averages (Mack, 2013; "No Choice," 2013; O'Connor, 2013).

Unionized teachers had numerous questions about charter schools. They posed them to Florida's legislators. They expected answers.

Ignoring Questions

Some politicians distrusted unionized teachers. They judged that they were too concerned about their salaries, benefits, and job security. The politicians concluded that the unionized teachers had irreconcilable conflicts of interest.

The politicians had little respect for unionized teachers. They resolved to ignore the questions that the teachers were posing about charter schools.

The politicians waited to see how people would respond to their tactics. They were not concerned about the teachers. However, they were concerned about influential allies of the teachers.

The politicians became nervous when the teachers' questions were repeated by their allies. They were particularly concerned when they were repeated by newspaper reporters and broadcast journalists.

The politicians conceded that many reporters and broadcasters sympathized with public-school teachers. They worried that the media would influence their readers, listeners, and viewers. They were especially worried about two key groups in this audience—parents and businesspeople.

Reactions

Parents and businesspeople listened carefully to the advocates for charter schools; they also listened to the critics. Many of them sympathized with the advocates.

Parents

Parents had practical reasons to sympathize with charter schools. They dreaded the difficulty of creating new public schools in their neighborhoods. They were ecstatic about the ease with which they could create charter schools (Hiaasen & McGrory, 2011).

Parents prized charter schools because of their academic reputations. They were assured that their students scored higher on standardized academic tests than the students at traditional public schools.

Parents prized charter schools because they kept students safe. They judged that they placed a higher priority on discipline and supervision than traditional public schools.

Parents prized charter schools because they had similarities to private schools. Many of the parents wished to send their children to private schools but could not afford the tuition. They viewed charter schools as publically funded proxies for the private schools.

Parents prized charter schools because they offered experiences similar to those at religious schools. They were impressed when church-located schools reconfigured as charter schools but remained in their ecclesiastical settings (M. Smith, 2013).

Businesspeople

Florida politicians were interested in the ways that key constituents reacted to charter schools. They were pleased with the reactions of many parents. However, they also wished to gauge how businesspeople were reacting.

Businesspeople generally were enthusiastic about charter schools. They had several reasons to support them.

Businesspeople had a philosophical reason to support charter schools. They noted that many of them were organized by entrepreneurs. They admired the entrepreneurs because they had transformed public education into a for-profit venture. They were confident that their capitalistic spirit would improve public education (Hiaasen & McGrory, 2011).

Businesspeople had a managerial reason to support charter schools. They were impressed that the schools used cost-saving labor practices. They judged that they were validating comparable practices in the private sector.

Businesspeople had another managerial reason to support charter schools. They were impressed that the schools paid high salaries and generous benefits to their leaders. They viewed them as validating private-sector practices (Giordano, 2012a, 2014).

EXAMINING PARTISAN QUESTIONS

People sometimes did not answer questions. They explained that they would not answer any that came from partisan groups. Politicians used this explanation to dodge questions about charter schools.

Activity 6.1

A philanthropist posed questions about Bowdoin College. How did groups respond?

Table 6.1 identifies two groups: parents of Bowdoin students and donors.

Complete the table by indicating the ways in which the groups responded to the philanthropist. You can use symbols.

Use the symbol – if the groups exhibited low confidence in the philanthropist. Use the symbol ± for moderate confidence and the symbol + for high confidence. As a final step, explain the bases for the symbols that you selected.

You can rely on the information in this chapter, additional information, or the information cited in the references. If you are reading this chapter with colleagues, you can confer with them.

Table 6.1. A Philanthropist Poses Questions about Bowdoin College

Groups	Response*	Explanation
Parents		
Donors		

*– Low
± Moderate
+ High

DO CHARTER SCHOOLS IMPROVE PUBLIC EDUCATION? 75

Activity 6.2

The president of Bowdoin College refused to answer partisan questions about his institution. How did groups respond?

Table 6.2 identifies two groups: parents of Bowdoin students and donors.

Complete the table by indicating the ways in which the groups responded to the president. You can use symbols.

Use the symbol − if the groups exhibited low confidence in him. Use the symbol ± for moderate confidence and the symbol + for high confidence. As a final step, explain the bases for the symbols that you selected.

Table 6.2. A President Refuses to Answer Questions about Bowdoin College

Groups	Response*	Explanation
Parents		
Donors		

*− Low
± Moderate
+ High

Activity 6.3

Teachers posed questions about Florida's charter schools. How did groups respond?

Table 6.3 identifies two Florida groups: parents and businesspeople.

Complete the table by indicating the ways in which the groups responded to the teachers. You can use symbols.

Use the symbol – if the groups exhibited low confidence in the teachers. Use the symbol ± for moderate confidence and the symbol + for high confidence. As a final step, explain the bases for the symbols that you selected.

Table 6.3. Florida Teachers Pose Questions about Charter Schools

Groups	Response*	Explanation
Parents		
Businesspeople		

*– Low
± Moderate
+ High

DO CHARTER SCHOOLS IMPROVE PUBLIC EDUCATION?

Activity 6.4

Florida politicians refused to answer partisan questions about charter schools. How did groups respond?

Table 6.4 identifies two Florida groups: parents and businesspeople.

Complete the table by indicating the ways in which the groups responded to the politicians. You can use symbols.

Use the symbol – if the groups exhibited low confidence in the politicians. Use the symbol ± for moderate confidence and the symbol + for high confidence. As a final step, explain the bases for the symbols that you selected.

Table 6.4. Florida Politicians Refuse to Answer Questions about Charter Schools

Groups	Response*	Explanation
Parents		
Businesspeople		

*– Low
± Moderate
+ High

SUMMARY

Politicians faced questions about charter schools. They stated that they would not answer those that came from partisan groups.

⑦
WHAT IS THE SECRET BEHIND ACCURATE PREDICTIONS?

[A publisher signed a] testing contract with Texas [for] half-a-billion dollars.

—Gail Collins, 2012

Texas [is] the birthplace of the student-testing movement.

—Stephanie Banchero & Arian Campo-Flores, 2013

[The] Texas Association of Business . . . believes [standardized scholastic] testing is worth every penny.

—Scott Friedman, 2013

We're testing too much [in Texas].

—David Anthony, quoted by Hibberd, 2013

Changes in the [Texas] testing program have been prompted by high failure rates.

—Terrence Stutz, 2013

> Bending to popular outrage . . . [Texas legislators cut mandatory] exams from 15 to 5.
>
> —Valerie Strauss, 2013a

> If you are concerned about your child's performance with [Texas-mandated] tests . . . you are not alone.
>
> —Bob Barnes & Becky Barnes, 2014

> Texas public schools have consistently ranked among the bottom five nationally in per-student spending.
>
> —Morgan Smith, 2014

Statistical experts made predictions about political elections. Assessment experts made them about scholastic tests. They were not always correct.

POLITICAL PREDICTIONS

Pollsters predicted which candidates would win political races. They had a great influence on the donations and votes that candidates received.

Journalists were eager to discover the pollsters' predictions. In fact, some of them hired their own pollsters.

Experts

Readers, listeners, and viewers wanted information about political contests in 2012. They particularly wanted it for the presidential race.

The executives at Fox News hired their own pollster, Dick Morris. They selected him because of his expertise in statistics.

Like the executives at Fox News, those at the *New York Times* hired a pollster. They selected Nate Silver, who was another expert statistician.

Morris and Silver posed questions to comparably sized and similarly stratified samples. They then predicted how the nation would vote.

Morris predicted that the Republican candidate, Mitt Romney, would win the election. He stated that he would win by a landslide.

WHAT IS THE SECRET BEHIND ACCURATE PREDICTIONS?

Silver predicted that the Democratic candidate, Barack Obama, would win the election. He added that he would win handily.

Journalists recognized that the two high-profile pollsters had made irreconcilable predictions. They were surprised when they stood by their predictions throughout the long campaign.

The journalists realized that only one of the pollsters could be right. They were eager to see how the election would end.

The pollsters also were anxious to learn how the election would end. Silver, the *New York Times* pollster, paid close attention as ballots were tabulated on election night. He soon realized that he had been correct (Cohn, 2013; Marcus & Davis, 2013).

When Silver was asked how he had been successful, he stated that he had made sound technical decisions about sampling and data analysis. He added that he had used expert discretion to form the questions that he posed to voters (Silver, 2012).

The journalists also questioned Morris, the Fox News pollster. They asked him why his prediction had been inaccurate.

Morris insisted that he had made sound technical decisions. However, he admitted that he had allowed his right-leaning political convictions to influence his polling questions. He stated that he had compounded this error by proclaiming his predictions at the "top of his lungs" ("Dick Morris to Piers," 2013).

Reactions

The executives at the *New York Times* published polls. They influenced whether voters would attend political rallies, display political signs, make donations to candidates, and cast ballots.

The executives at the *New York Times* had circulated Silver's predictions for months. They were relieved when they turned out to be correct. They realized that these predictions had validated their paper as well as Silver (Noveck, 2012).

The polls circulated by Fox News influenced that station's viewers. They influenced whether they would attend political rallies, display political signs, make donations to candidates, and cast ballots.

The Fox News executives were chagrined when Morris turned out to be wrong. They judged that he had compromised his own credibility and that of their news organization. They did not conceal their displeasure: they fired him (Patten, 2013).

EDUCATIONAL PREDICTIONS

George W. Bush became governor of Texas in 1994. He was aware that the state's schools had two major problems: they were underfunded and underperforming. He planned to solve both problems simultaneously.

Bush promised to give schools the opportunity to earn financial rewards. Moreover, he pledged to provide the rewards without increasing the state's education budget. He explained that he was going to redistribute the current budget in a way that fostered competition.

Bush identified standardized testing as the key to his plan. He would channel funds to those schools at which students demonstrated high scores on tests. He even would channel them to schools at which students demonstrated improved scores. However, he would steer money away from the other schools.

Bush predicted that the winners in this competition would benefit: they would have additional funds. He predicted that even the losers would benefit: they would realize that the competition was academically regenerative. He asked the legislators to approve his plan ("Stats about School," 2012).

The Texas legislators were excited by Bush's plan. More than a decade later, they still were excited about it. Nonetheless, they thought they could improve it by designating a different set of tests.

The Texas legislators prescribed new high-stakes tests for all elementary, middle, and secondary schools in 2007. They gave the tests a cumbersome title: the *State of Texas Assessments of Academic Readiness*. They referred to them by the acronym *STAAR*.

Texas parents already knew about high-stakes tests: their children had to pass four of them to graduate from high school. Nonetheless, they were startled when they learned about the new tests: children would have to pass fifteen of them to graduate.

The parents created a ruckus. They made it clear to their school administrators that they opposed the STAAR battery. They asked them to make changes to it. They were disappointed when the administrators retorted that they were helpless. They decided to go directly to their legislators.

The legislators were startled by the intensity of the anti-STAAR parents. However, they hoped that their fervor would be counterbalanced by that of pro-STAAR allies. They expected Texas employers to become staunch allies. They were correct.

The employers had been grumbling about students' deficiencies in mathematics, reading, writing, physical sciences, social sciences, algebra, and geometry. They saw STAAR as a way to document those deficiencies.

Experts

The Pearson Corporation is the largest scholastic testing company in the United States. Its executives strongly endorsed the legislative changes to the Texas testing plan. In fact, they had collaborated with the legislators.

The executives at Pearson were excited because STAAR was innovative; they also were excited because it was supported by a half-billion-dollar budget. They were sure that they would receive the contract (Collins, 2012).

Assessment professionals who did not work at Pearson had no chance of winning the STAAR contract. Nonetheless, even they were excited. They anticipated that STAAR would create a large and lucrative market in test preparation. They were ready to develop materials and provide services for this market ("STAAR Practice," 2013; "Texas STAAR," 2013).

Reactions

Legislators had guaranteed that STAAR would improve instruction and learning. They made an impression on parents, who were comforted by their assurances.

Not all parents were enthusiastic about STAAR. Some of them were wary. They demanded additional information.

The skeptical parents asked the legislators to predict how children would score on STAAR. They were disappointed when the legislators declined.

The legislators explained that they could not make a prediction until the test was developed. They reckoned that this process would take five years.

STAAR was ready in 2012. Sample questions from it were released that spring.

After reviewing the sample questions, teachers made a prediction. They predicted that their students would do poorly on it. They explained that they would struggle because the questions in the test were not aligned with the content in courses.

The teachers had other reasons to be pessimistic. They feared that the test's eccentrically formatted questions would confuse students. They were concerned that its excessive length would fatigue them ("Top Ten Problems," 2013).

The assessment experts at Pearson made their own prediction. They predicted that the students' scores on STAAR would decline, but only slightly from those on earlier tests. They reasoned that a modest decline was inevitable because STAAR was more rigorous than the tests it replaced.

Parents realized that the teachers and the assessment experts had made very different predictions. They wondered which group was correct. They were eager to learn the actual test results.

The parents eventually did see scores. They were shocked when they discovered that the scores had plunged to a point where they would block many students from graduating. They wanted to know how the experts could have missed this consequence (Hibberd, 2013; "Strong Showing," 2013).

Testing enthusiasts could not explain why the experts had miscalculated. Nonetheless, they insisted that the test was appropriate. They warned legislators that any changes to it would harm students, schools, employers, and the entire nation (Cook & Moore, 2013).

The legislators were not cowed by the testing enthusiasts. They told the enthusiasts that they, the legislators, had lost confidence in STAAR. They added that they were ready to modify it (Farah, 2013; Harris, 2013; Smith, 2012).

EXAMINING SPECULATIVE QUESTIONS

Statistical experts sometimes had difficulty predicting the results of political elections. Assessment experts sometimes had difficulty predicting the results of scholastic tests.

WHAT IS THE SECRET BEHIND ACCURATE PREDICTIONS? 85

Activity 7.1

A Fox News pollster predicted that the Republican candidate would win the 2012 presidential election. How did groups respond?

Table 7.1 identifies two groups: voters and Fox News executives.

Complete the table by indicating the ways in which the groups responded to the pollster. You can use symbols.

Use the symbol − if the groups exhibited low confidence in him. Use the symbol ± for moderate confidence and the symbol + for high confidence. As a final step, explain the bases for the symbols that you selected.

You can rely on the information in this chapter, additional information, or the information cited in the references. If you are reading this chapter with colleagues, you can confer with them.

Table 7.1. A Fox News Pollster Makes Political Predictions

Groups	Response*	Explanation
Voters		
Executives—Fox News		

*− Low
± Moderate
+ High

Activity 7.2

A *New York Times* pollster predicted that the Democratic candidate would win the 2012 presidential election. How did groups respond?

Table 7.2 identifies two groups: voters and *New York Times* executives.

Complete the table by indicating the ways in which the groups responded to the pollster. You can use symbols.

Use the symbol – if the groups exhibited low confidence in him. Use the symbol ± for moderate confidence and the symbol + for high confidence. As a final step, explain the bases for the symbols that you selected.

Table 7.2. A *New York Times* Pollster Makes Political Predictions

Groups	Response*	Explanation
Voters		
Executives—*Times*		

*– Low
± Moderate
+ High

WHAT IS THE SECRET BEHIND ACCURATE PREDICTIONS? 87

Activity 7.3

Assessment experts at Pearson predicted that scores on STAAR would decline only slightly from those on prior state tests. How did groups respond?

Table 7.3 identifies two Texas groups: parents and state legislators.

Complete the table by indicating the ways in which the groups responded to the Pearson experts. You can use symbols.

Use the symbol – if the groups exhibited low confidence in the experts. Use the symbol ± for moderate confidence and the symbol + for high confidence. As a final step, explain the bases for the symbols that you selected.

Table 7.3. Assessment Experts Make Predictions about STAAR

Groups	Response*	Explanation
Parents		
Legislators		

*– Low
± Moderate
+ High

Activity 7.4

Texas teachers predicted that scores on STAAR would decline dramatically from those on prior state tests. How did groups respond?

Table 7.4 identifies two Texas groups: parents and state legislators.

Complete the table by indicating the ways in which the groups responded to the Texas teachers. You can use symbols.

Use the symbol – if the groups exhibited low confidence in the teachers. Use the symbol ± for moderate confidence and the symbol + for high confidence. As a final step, explain the bases for the symbols that you selected.

Table 7.4. Texas Teachers Make Predictions about STAAR

Groups	Response*	Explanation
Parents		
Legislators		

*– Low
± Moderate
+ High

SUMMARY

Statistical experts made predictions about political elections. Assessment experts made them about scholastic tests. They were not always accurate.

8

ARE TEXTBOOKS POLITICAL?

Battles over textbooks are nothing new . . . in Texas.

—Mariah Blake, 2010

Texas [adopts] . . . slanted . . . social studies books.

—"Texas Textbooks," 2010

Texas school districts are able to buy books that the state board rejects . . . but they'll have to use their own money.

—Michael Birnbaum, 2010

Hundreds . . . traveled to Austin . . . to testify . . . [about] textbooks.

—Rebecca Klein, 2013

[Texas] parents . . . say the authors of a [text]book . . . misfired when they defined the Second Amendment.

—Edmund DeMarche, 2013

In order to review the large number of [social studies] textbooks [submitted to Texas], we need hundreds of volunteer reviewers.

—Barbara Cargill, quoted by Alexander, 2014

Investors expressed financial views to influence stock sales. Scholastic publishers expressed political views to influence book sales.

HERBALIFE

Herbalife manufactures diet aids, vitamins, and health goods that are hardly novel. However, it distributes them in a fashion that is highly distinctive.

Millions of part-time sales agents sell Herbalife products. They peddle them to their relatives, neighbors, social acquaintances, and workplace colleagues.

The sales agents keep a portion of the cash from each transaction. They increase their earnings by recruiting new distributors; they retain a portion of the cash that new recruits generate.

The Herbalife executives boast that their corporation has a multilevel marketing compensation structure. They contend that this infrastructure is minimal but that it still provides high incentives to sales agents.

Skeptics describe the Herbalife infrastructure with a less flattering term: they call it a pyramid. They note that the closer that the sales agents are to the apex, the more money they make.

A hedge-fund investor was skeptical of Herbalife's finances; he insisted that they were fundamentally unsound. He used speeches, interviews, and website postings to express this view (Schmidt, Lipton, & Stevenson, 2014).

Even though the investor questioned the value of Herbalife shares, he bought a billion dollars of them. He purchased them on credit with the intention of selling them short. He explained that he would sell them at their current, inflated price and then replace them after their price had sunk ("Ackman Goes," 2013; Chung, 2013a; La Roche, 2012).

The executives at Herbalife fumed at the skeptical investor. They stated that he deliberately expressed views that would cause the prices of shares to drop. They claimed that his sole goal was to make a quick profit.

The Herbalife executives became anxious as the prices of shares declined. They believed that their antagonist's plan was working. Although they fretted for weeks, they eventually were able to breathe a sigh of relief.

Two influential investors publicly proclaimed their confidence in Herbalife. These investors represented large and powerful hedge funds. They stated that they would demonstrate their confidence by purchasing a massive block of shares (Chapman, 2013; Russolillo, 2013).

The two investors declared that they intended to sell their shares long: they would trade them after a relatively extended period. They were sure that the shares would grow in value during that period.

Journalists were intrigued by the investors; they wrote at length about their feud. They assumed that only one side could prevail. They were surprised when both sides had the opportunities to garner huge profits (Jenkins, 2013; Salmon, 2012).

One investor had predicted that the Herbalife shares would become cheaper. He was correct. After buying shares at high prices, he sold them immediately. He later had the chance to purchase cheaper shares, use them to satisfy his debt, and pocket the multimillion-dollar difference.

The rival investors purchased Herbalife shares after prices had plummeted. Because they restored confidence in the corporation, they caused prices to increase. As a result, they also had the chance to make millions of dollars (Chung, 2013b).

SOCIAL STUDIES TEXTBOOKS

Publishers hoped that their textbooks would be adopted widely. They had especially high hopes for their social studies textbooks, which they marketed to every school in the country.

The publishers speculated about the features that they should incorporate into their social studies textbooks. They frequently examined bestselling series of books and then extrapolated their features into their own materials.

The publishers realized that illustrations heavily influenced textbook sales. They filled their books with etchings, graphs, line maps, two-tone photos, and color pictures.

Publishers recognized that covers also influenced sales. Most of them chose hardcovers, which made their books sturdy enough to be passed from one group of students to the next. Nonetheless, some chose soft covers, which made books lighter and less expensive (Giordano, 2003).

The publishers considered every aspect of social studies textbooks. They agonized about the ways in which fonts, margins, page sizes, and paper textures could affect sales.

Publishers eventually had to make a drastic decision about textbooks: they had to decide whether to convert them into e-textbooks. E-textbooks saved money because they did not require paper, warehousing, or shipping. They also saved money because the content in them could be tailored inexpensively to satisfy opinionated customers (Giordano, 2012a).

Content

Parents were concerned about the content in social studies textbooks; they did not hesitate to give the publishers their advice. They were upset when the publishers ignored them.

Parents also went to teachers, school administrators, and school board members. They told them why they disapproved of textbook content. However, they often were disappointed with the way in which school personnel responded. They therefore took their complaints to politicians (Giordano, 2003, 2009).

Politicians did not ignore the disgruntled parents; in fact, they were eager to placate them. They created state panels to make judgments about the content in the social studies textbooks. They then appointed the parents to these panels. They assured the parents that they would provide state funds only for those textbooks that were panel-approved (Giordano, 2003; Klein, 2013).

American Exceptionalism

Parents had explicit expectations for textbooks; many of them expected them to be patriotic. They explained that they should honor America's leaders, legal system, military, economy, and foreign policies. Some of them had an additional expectation: they should highlight *American Exceptionalism* ("As Governor," 2013).

American Exceptionalism has recently attracted a lot of attention. However, it is not a novel ideological concept. It was popular during the nineteenth century, when it was tied to another concept: *manifest destiny* (Edwards & Weiss, 2011; Gingrich & Haley, 2011).

Manifest destiny asserted that the United States had the right to amass territory beyond its borders. American Exceptionalism was less strident; it asserted that the nation had an obligation to exercise leadership beyond its borders (Hodgson, 2009; Ignatieff, 2005).

Many politicians stated that they subscribed to American Exceptionalism. Even President Obama expressed carefully qualified support for it (Madhani, 2013).

Publishers wanted to market their textbooks efficiently. They looked for a way to identify those school districts that would be interested in books that featured American Exceptionalism. For example, they assumed that districts would be interested if their school administrators or school board members organized conferences about American Exceptionalism (Stepzinski, 2013).

The publishers also wanted to identify the states that would be interested in books that featured American Exceptionalism. They therefore examined the social studies standards for individual states. They noted that the standards for some states, such as Texas, revealed a strong commitment to American Exceptionalism (Blake, 2010; Giordano, 2003; "Texas Textbooks," 2010).

Common Core

Scholastic publishers hoped that the political views expressed within their social studies textbooks would lure customers. They sometimes featured viewpoints that would appeal to politically conservative customers; they sometimes featured viewpoints that would appeal to politically liberal customers. They recognized that both customer groups influenced textbook purchases.

Scholastic publishers looked for additional ways to lure customers to social studies textbooks. Some of them detected an opportunity with the Common Core (Turner, 2014).

The publishers characterized the Common Core as a compendium of key information that all students should master. They assumed that textbooks that were aligned with it would be popular.

The publishers were aware that the politicians in some states opposed the Common Core. For example, they noted that those in Texas had characterized it as a federal intrusion into local schools. They expected them to avoid textbooks that were aligned with the Common Core.

In spite of resistance from Texas and several other states, publishers expected to sell many of the textbooks that they aligned with the Common Core. After all, the Common Core had been developed by a politically bipartisan group. They were convinced that it appealed to both conservative and liberal customers.

When the publishers announced that they would align social studies textbooks with the Common Core, they were not anticipating that parents would fuss. They were shocked when many of them became angry.

Parents were angry at the publishers. However, they were even angrier with the politicians who had endorsed the Common Core. They urged them to change their minds. Parents were relieved when those in Indiana, Louisiana, South Carolina, and Oklahoma indicated that they were having second thoughts.

The politicians explained why they were changing their minds. Some of them agreed with their Texas colleagues: they worried that the Common Core was a federal initiative to regulate textbook content. They argued that textbook content should be left to states and local communities (DeMarche, 2013; Swasey, 2013).

Some politicians judged that the Common Core focused too heavily on politically liberal viewpoints. They concluded that it suppressed conservative views, including those about American Exceptionalism (Carlson, 2013; "Maryland Police," 2013).

Some politicians claimed that the Common Core had uncertain pedagogical consequences. For example, they were unsure how children would score on tests that were geared to it.

Politicians acceded to the advice from their constituents. They withdrew their endorsements of the Common Core and the textbooks that were synchronized to it (Banchero, 2013; Brooks, 2013c; Dixon, 2013).

EXAMINING POLITICIZED QUESTIONS

High-powered investors expressed their financial views about stocks; they hoped that they would affect sales. Publishers expressed political views within social studies textbooks; they hoped that they would affect sales.

Activity 8.1

A prominent investor announced that he would purchase Herbalife shares, retain them briefly, and sell them short. How did groups respond?

Table 8.1 identifies two groups: executives at Herbalife and stock market traders.

Complete the table by indicating the ways in which the groups responded to the investor. You can use symbols.

Use the symbol – if the groups had low confidence in the investor. Use the symbol ± for moderate confidence and the symbol + for high confidence. As a final step, explain the bases for the symbols that you selected.

You can rely on the information in this chapter, additional information, or the information cited in the references. If you are reading this chapter with colleagues, you can confer with them.

Table 8.1. An Investor Sells Herbalife Stocks Short

Groups	Response*	Explanation
Executives		
Traders		

*– Low
± Moderate
+ High

Activity 8.2

Two prominent investors announced that they would purchase Herbalife shares, retain them for an extended period, and then sell them long. How did groups respond?

Table 8.2 identifies two groups: executives at Herbalife and stock market traders.

Complete the table by indicating the ways in which the groups responded to the two investors. You can use symbols.

Use the symbol – if the groups had low confidence in the investors. Use the symbol ± for moderate confidence and the symbol + for high confidence. As a final step, explain the bases for the symbols that you selected.

Table 8.2. Investors Sell Herbalife Stocks Long

Groups	Response*	Explanation
Executives		
Traders		

*– Low
± Moderate
+ High

Activity 8.3

Publishers aligned textbooks with American Exceptionalism. How did groups respond?

Table 8.3 identifies two groups: politicians and parents.

Complete the table by indicating the ways in which the groups responded to the publishers. You can use symbols.

Use the symbol – if the groups had low confidence in the publishers. Use the symbol ± for moderate confidence and the symbol + for high confidence. As a final step, explain the bases for the symbols that you selected.

Table 8.3. Publishers Align Textbooks with American Exceptionalism

Groups	Response*	Explanation
Politicians		
Parents		

*– Low
± Moderate
+ High

Activity 8.4

Publishers aligned textbooks with the Common Core. How did groups respond?

Table 8.4 identifies two groups: politicians and parents.

Complete the table by indicating the ways in which the groups responded to the publishers. You can use symbols.

Use the symbol – if the groups had low confidence in the publishers. Use the symbol ± for moderate confidence and the symbol + for high confidence. As a final step, explain the bases for the symbols that you selected.

Table 8.4. Publishers Align Textbooks with the Common Core

Groups	Response*	Explanation
Politicians		
Parents		

*– Low
± Moderate
+ High

SUMMARY

Investors expressed their financial views in ways that would influence stock sales. They made an impression on publishers, who used political views to influence textbook sales.

9

HOW SHOULD PRINCIPALS BE RECRUITED?

Elimination of [administrative] tenure . . . would mean exposing principals to the worst kind of political pressures.

—Ted Elsberg, 1988

Principals . . . drive student learning.

—Karin Chenoweth, 2012

How do principals really improve schools?

—Rick DuFour & Mike Mattos, 2013

The principal [is] the most misunderstood person in all of education.

—Kate Rousmaniere, 2013

If the principal does not return your phone calls . . . contact the superintendent.

—"What to Do," 2013

> A state investigation . . . found that . . . principals . . . cheated [on standardized tests].
>
> —Richard Fausset, 2014

> We will use progressive discipline [with principals].
>
> —Superintendent Nikolai Vitti, quoted by Stepzinski, 2014

Corporate boards came up with strategies to recruit dynamic leaders. They made an impression on school boards, which also were trying to recruit dynamic leaders.

BUSINESS LEADERS

Boards of directors hoped that their corporations would prosper. The boards of American and British automotive corporations were exultant in the middle of the twentieth century: profits had risen to dizzying heights.

The boards looked for the persons to whom they should give credit for their firms' success. They singled out the top executives (Freeland, 2001; Mullins, 2006).

Automotive profits eventually declined. In fact, they plunged precipitously. During this troublesome era, boards looked for persons to blame. They once again singled out top executives.

Recruitment Strategies

Boards of directors wished to hire effective executives. They hoped to attract individuals who were bold, independent, visionary, and risk-taking (Freeland, 2001; Mullins, 2006).

The boards did not think that they would have trouble locating candidates who would become exemplary executives. However, they were not sure that they could persuade candidates to accept the jobs in their organizations. They needed a way to lure them.

Bonuses

The boards tried to entice candidates with bonuses. They promised them chances to earn mammoth and even colossal cash awards ("Executive Pay," 2012).

Boards of directors followed through on their promise. They revealed their commitment in the way that they treated the executives at top New York securities firms. In 2012, they gave each executive an average bonus of twenty million dollars (Philbin, 2013).

The boards had anticipated that executives would be excited about mammoth bonuses. They failed to anticipate how business journalists would respond.

Some of the journalists were unenthusiastic about bonuses. They complained that they were indefensibly large.

The journalists even questioned whether the bonuses were deserved. They pointed out that the bonuses were tied to the corporate profitability reports that the executives supplied. They suspected that executives had tailored those reports to maximize their bonuses (Mintzberg, 2012).

Many persons showed interest in journalistic exposés of executive bonuses. Some of them demanded action: they urged the corporate boards to change their practices.

Severance Guarantees

Boards of directors listened as journalists and their audiences complained about costly bonuses. Although the boards may have been stung by their criticism, they insisted that they would retain the bonuses. In fact, they wished to supplement them with still another expensive enticement.

The boards explained that they wished to entice candidates who had the temperaments to make bold decisions. They realized that these candidates, once they became executives, could hesitate to announce bold decisions that would arouse corporate factions and jeopardize their jobs.

The boards came up with a way to reassure executives who were nervous about being dismissed. They guaranteed them that they would receive extremely generous severance packages (Klein, P., 2007; "End of Exorbitant," 2012).

The boards anticipated that executives would be enthusiastic about generous severance packages. They anticipated that some persons would react critically. They braced for the reactions of journalists.

Many journalists were critical. They gave examples of executives who were fired but who were awarded hundreds of millions of dollars in severance payments. They publicized one case in which an executive was retained for a single day, dismissed, and then awarded forty-four million dollars in severance pay ("CEO Gets Cool," 2012; Flannery, 2012).

Readers, listeners, and viewers were interested in disclosures about enormous severance packages. Some of them were more than interested; they were outraged.

Corporate boards were unfazed. They stated that they had complete confidence in the severance packages. They revealed their confidence in 2011; they gave the departing executives at elite firms about twenty million dollars each in severance (Weigley, 2011).

The boards devised an ingenious rationalization for generous severance packages. They explained that dismissed executives, who typically received a portion of their severance package in stock shares, had taken steps to maximize the value of those shares. They concluded that both the executives and the shareholders benefited from this arrangement (Graham, Roth, & Dugan, 2008; Lipman & Hall, 2008; Rosenthal, 2012).

Journalists were not swayed by the boards' logic. They countered with examples of CEOs who had made injudicious decisions, damaged shareholders, merited dismissal, and then walked away with lucrative severance packages (Bebchuk & Fried, 2004; "CEOs with Severance Packages," 2011; Dash, 2011).

SCHOOL LEADERS

School boards were cheerful when their districts excelled; they were sour when the districts languished. In both cases, they looked for the persons who were responsible. They frequently focused on school administrators.

School boards appreciated their superintendents. They noted that superintendents were responsible for districts' strategic goals. They realized that superintendents had multiple opportunities to set, implement, monitor, and fine-tune those goals.

School boards also appreciated their principals. They judged that principals were directly accountable for students' day-to-day learning. Moreover, they realized that principals had many opportunities to influence students' learning (Kowalski, 2010; Nelson & Sassi, 2005; Stronge, Richard, & Catano, 2008).

Principals could influence learning when they interacted with students; they also could influence it when they interacted with teachers, nonteaching professionals, and support staffs. The most effective principals were attentive to all of these inside-the-schools groups.

Principals even could influence learning during their interactions with outside-the-schools groups. They could influence it during routine meetings with parents; they might influence it during occasional meetings with politicians, employers, and union representatives (Banchero, 2012; Brown, 2012; "Whatever Means Necessary," 2012).

Recruitment Strategies

School boards prized effective leaders. However, they needed strategies to recruit them. They were impressed by the strategies of the corporate boards.

Bonuses

Corporate boards paid generous bonuses to executives. They contended that the opportunity to earn these awards persuaded superior candidates to join their firms.

The school boards gave large bonuses to their superintendents. However, they became nervous after they were criticized for being too extravagant (Brody, 2014).

The school boards were not ready to give large bonuses to principals. However, they were willing to pay modest bonuses to them.

The members of the New York City school board approved principal bonuses in 2001. They gave fifteen thousand dollars to hundreds of individuals.

The members of the school board waited to see how their city's journalists would respond to the bonuses. They were relieved when they did not protest. They were even more pleased when their readers, listeners, and viewers were unperturbed. They decided to continue making modest payments.

The New York City school board raised the cap on principals' bonuses to twenty-five thousand dollars in 2012. It made an impression on Chicago's school board, which awarded twenty-thousand-dollar bonuses to its principals (Cramer, 2012; Hartocollis, 2001; Phillips, 2012; Spielman, 2012).

School boards believed that opportunities to earn bonuses persuaded high-quality applicants to become principals. However, they wished to experiment with an additional enticement: they wanted to offer signing bonuses (Gootmans, 2004).

Not all of the school boards gave signing bonuses. Some of them could not afford them. Others were prevented by state laws.

The school boards that did offer signing bonuses had to be careful to stay within legally set boundaries. For example, boards in the state of Washington could offer signing bonuses only if they did not exceed twenty-eight thousand dollars ("Union Concerned," 2012).

Severance Guarantees

School boards judged that administrative candidates would be excited by bonuses. They judged that they would be even more excited if they were protected from damaging dismissals.

School boards already had offered protection from dismissal to superintendents. They had copied the corporate practice of generous severance packages. Although they had confidence in these packages, they were nervous because of the uproar that had accompanied them. They were not ready to offer similar packages to principals (Capps, 2011; Clayton, 2012; Kingsbury, 2012; Rado & Eldeib, 2011; Stiles, 2011).

School boards looked for another way to assure candidates that they would not have to fear reprisal from powerful, factionalized constituents. They decided to offer administrative tenure to them.

Administrative tenure guaranteed that principals would remain in their current positions or be transferred to comparable positions. It also guaranteed that principals would retain their salaries and employment benefits.

Principal candidates were intrigued by administrative tenure. They were enthusiastic as well.

Like the principals, journalists were intrigued by administrative tenure. However, they were not enthusiastic.

The journalists conceded that administrative tenure could protect bold and visionary principals. They noted that it also could protect complacent and narrow-minded bureaucrats (Elsberg, 1988; "Ending Tenure for Principals," 1999).

The journalists were skeptical of administrative tenure for another reason: they detected de facto versions of it. They explained that districts without explicit administrative tenure policies were allowing individuals to retain positions for their entire careers. Journalists demanded changes to these practices. They urged the public to join with them (Ripp, 2012).

School boards were nervous when journalists and the public criticized policies for recruiting, retaining, and dismissing principals. Under pressure, they agreed to make changes.

School boards stated that they would appoint principals for limited terms. They added that they would remove ineffective principals even before their terms had ended. They noted that principals would be classified as ineffective if they were assigned to schools with low test scores and failed to raise the scores.

Politicians already were getting rid of teachers who failed to raise low test scores; they were excited about using the same procedure to get rid of principals. They assumed that qualified individuals would be eager to compete for the principals' jobs. They later were surprised at the few who showed interest (Dillon, 2011; Stuit, 2010).

EXAMINING MANAGERIAL QUESTIONS

Corporate boards tried to recruit bold leaders with bonuses and severance packages. They made an impression on school boards, which also were trying to recruit bold leaders.

Activity 9.1

Corporate boards tried to recruit executives through enormous bonuses. How did groups respond?

Table 9.1 identifies two groups: journalists and members of the public.

Complete the table by indicating the ways in which groups responded to the corporate boards. You can use symbols.

Use the symbol – if groups had low confidence in the corporate boards. Use the symbol ± for moderate confidence and the symbol + for high confidence. As a final step, explain the bases for the symbols that you selected.

You can rely on the information in this chapter, additional information, or the information cited in the references. If you are reading this chapter with colleagues, you can confer with them.

Table 9.1. Corporate Boards Offer Enormous Bonuses

Groups	Response*	Explanation
Journalists		
Public		

*– Low
± Moderate
+ High

HOW SHOULD PRINCIPALS BE RECRUITED?

Activity 9.2

Corporate boards tried to recruit executives through generous severance packages. How did groups respond?

Table 9.2 identifies two groups: journalists and members of the public.

Complete the table by indicating the ways in which groups responded to the corporate boards. You can use symbols.

Use the symbol – if groups had low confidence in the corporate boards. Use the symbol ± for moderate confidence and the symbol + for high confidence. As a final step, explain the bases for the symbols that you selected.

Table 9.2. Corporate Boards Offer Generous Severance Packages

Groups	Response*	Explanation
Journalists		
Public		

*– Low
± Moderate
+ High

Activity 9.3

School boards tried to recruit principals through modest bonuses. How did groups respond?

Table 9.3 identifies two groups: journalists and members of the public.

Complete the table by indicating the ways in which groups responded to the school boards. You can use symbols.

Use the symbol – if groups had low confidence in the school boards. Use the symbol ± for moderate confidence and the symbol + for high confidence. As a final step, explain the bases for the symbols that you selected.

Table 9.3. School Boards Offer Modest Bonuses

Groups	Response*	Explanation
Journalists		
Public		

*– Low
± Moderate
+ High

HOW SHOULD PRINCIPALS BE RECRUITED?

Activity 9.4

School boards tried to recruit principals through administrative tenure. How did groups respond?

Table 9.4 identifies two groups: journalists and members of the public.

Complete the table by indicating the ways in which groups responded to the school boards. You can use symbols.

Use the symbol – if groups had low confidence in the school boards. Use the symbol ± for moderate confidence and the symbol + for high confidence. As a final step, explain the bases for the symbols that you selected.

Table 9.4. School Boards Offer Administrative Tenure

Groups	Response*	Explanation
Journalists		
Public		

*– Low
± Moderate
+ High

SUMMARY

Corporate boards devised strategies to recruit bold leaders. They made an impression on school boards, which modified their strategies.

10

CAN SIMPLE SOLUTIONS ELIMINATE COMPLEX PROBLEMS?

The school year is too short.

    —Secretary of Education Arne Duncan, quoted by Holland, 2009

[A longer school year is] going to cost some money.

    —Barack Obama, quoted by Sisk & Siemaszko, 2010

Five states . . . will add . . . time to the [school] calendar.

    —Josh Lederman, 2012

Adding hours to the school day has become a . . . mantra of . . . corporate education.

    —John Spencer, 2013

Some teachers want [a] longer school year because they're . . . judged on how much students learn.

    —Molly Bloom, 2013

The summer learning slide . . . costs on average two to three months of learning.

    —Aly Seidel, 2014

Groups proffered solutions for complex problems. They may have had ulterior motives when they proffered extremely simple solutions.

NATIONAL DEFENSE

Stanley Kubrick released a controversial film in 1964. He gave it a terse title, *Dr. Strangelove*. However, he added a meandering subtitle, *How I Learned to Stop Worrying and Love the Bomb* (Kubrick, 2001).

The film depicted a nuclear catastrophe. Even though it was obviously fictional and frequently farcical, it engrossed Cold War viewers (Renaker, 2000).

At a climactic moment in the film, an American president assembled his national security team. He informed the group that the United States and the Soviet Union had launched nuclear missiles against each other. He lamented that the weapons, which could not be halted, would annihilate mankind.

A member of the security team interrupted the president. He announced that the federal government had anticipated this crisis, constructed a massive fallout shelter, and was ready to transport the president and other key leaders to this nearby facility. He was confident that they all would be safe.

During the Cold War, members of the federal government actually had constructed a fallout shelter similar to the one in the film. However, they were not the sole group to build shelters. Local agents had placed them in civic centers, airports, and schools. Businesspeople had placed them in stadiums, arenas, office buildings, apartment houses, and even single-family residences ("Apartment Approved," 1961; Churney, 2008; "Hidden in Plain View," 2000).

Citizens were relieved that they had access to fallout shelters. Nonetheless, they wondered whether these shelters had been constructed with sufficient care. They wanted a way to assess their safety (Monteyne, 2011).

Federal bureaucrats supplied the public with fallout-shelter building codes: they highlighted the dimensions, features, locations, and construction materials of safe shelters. They also identified the supplies with which the shelters were to be equipped: generators, fuel, canned foods, blankets, water, medicine, tools, flashlights, batteries, portable toilets, radiation monitors, radios, and books (Rose, 2001).

Many citizens commended federal politicians for distributing information about fallout shelters. They assumed that the politicians wished to safeguard the nation. However, some persons suspected that the politicians had ulterior motives. Journalists and political analysts were highly skeptical.

The skeptics realized that nuclear attacks entailed complex threats. They were struck by the simplicity of the proposal to neutralize the threats through shelters.

The skeptics judged that the shelters evoked two distinct emotions. They made citizens feel safe from nuclear threats. However, they simultaneously made citizens feel apprehensive about the horrifying consequences of those threats.

The skeptics concluded that politicians deliberately wished to stoke public fear. They explained that they were using it as the pretext for steering resources to the military, local electoral districts, and friendly defense contractors (Roy, 2010).

SCHOOL CALENDARS

Early school administrators had to make genuinely critical decisions. They had to hire teachers, build schoolhouses, purchase equipment, designate learning materials, arrange student transportation, assemble curricula, and select pedagogy.

The early school administrators also had to make somewhat bureaucratic decisions. They had to order office supplies, designate maintenance schedules, supervise auxiliary staffs, complete district reports, and monitor compliance with state directives.

The school administrators usually agreed about the tasks that should be categorized as critical and those that should be categorized as bureaucratic. Nonetheless, they occasionally could not agree. They could not agree about school calendars.

All of the school administrators realized that they had to create a calendar. However, novice administrators and experienced administrators viewed this task differently.

The novice administrators assumed that the calendar would be simple and noncontroversial. They judged that it was one of the many bureaucratic tasks to which they had to be attentive.

Experienced school administrators realized that creating a school calendar could be complex and contentious. They knew that it sometimes became the most important task for which they were responsible.

African American Students

The early administrators had to specify the dates on which schools would begin and end. Those in Northern states took a straightforward approach: they established a common calendar for all of their students (Giordano, 2009).

The administrators in the South had to establish calendars for segregated schools. They decided to take a race-based approach: they established one calendar for black schools and a different one for white schools. They typically made the calendar for black schools two to six weeks shorter than the one for white schools (Giordano, 2009; Snyder, 1993).

Administrators in the South implemented race-based scholastic calendars after the Civil War. They continued to use them during the nineteenth century and throughout the first half of the subsequent century. Some were still using them during the 1970s (Giordano, 2009).

The administrators in the South came up with reasons to give African American students shorter school calendars. Some of them were convinced that they would not benefit from more time in school.

To control spending, some school administrators shortened the calendars for African American students. They realized that they would spend less on instructional personnel, student transportation, and building utilities (Giordano, 2009; Mitchell, 2010).

Some school administrators shortened the calendars of African American students to create cheap field labor. They realized that local farmers counted on these students to help with spring planting (Margo, 1990; Miller, 1995).

Some school administrators shortened the calendars of African American students to appease insecure white parents. The white parents, who were threatened by the economic and political advances of African Americans, wished to create obstacles. They judged that a shorter school calendar could constitute a particularly troublesome impediment for African American children (Giordano, 2009).

Students with Disabilities

All schoolchildren faced problems. Nonetheless, those with disabilities faced enormously difficult problems. For example, they frequently forgot over the summer much of the learning that they had acquired during the school year.

Advocates for students with disabilities had a suggestion to improve learning: they urged school administrators to provide year-round instruction. Anticipating that the school administrators might be unwilling to make this change, they had a pragmatic alternative. They simply could extend school calendars.

The school administrators were reluctant to make any calendar changes for students with disabilities. They acknowledged that these students regressed during summer vacations. However, they pointed out that other students regressed as well. They questioned whether schools could equitably lengthen the calendar for only one group.

School administrators were concerned about the equity of a longer school calendar; they also were concerned about the expense. They stated that they did not have the funds to pay for this calendar change.

Advocates for students with disabilities did not give up; they asked parents to help them. They urged parents to demand an extended school year for their children.

The parents made their demands to school administrators. When they did not detect any progress, they decided to recruit allies. Although they recruited physicians, social workers, and police officers, they still made little progress (Giordano, 2007).

Parents eventually made their demands to the courts. They argued that effective education, which was a civil right of children with disabilities, should entail year-round schooling. They were overjoyed when judges agreed with them (Giordano, 2007; Norlin, 2008).

Parents also made their demands to federal lawmakers. They asked them to mandate a longer school year for students with severe disabilities. They even asked them to pay a portion of the costs. They were excited when the lawmakers acceded to both demands.

All Students

School administrators were upset when they were forced to provide year-round programs for students with disabilities. They worried that they would be forced to provide them for many more students. Their worries were realistic.

Some enthusiasts requested that the administrators make year-round schooling available to all students. When they realized that the administrators were resistant, they tried to exert pressure on them. They went to their legislators for assistance.

Enthusiasts began to plead with their legislators for longer school calendars during the 1960s. Although they had little success, they did not give up. They entreated them for decades; they still are entreating them today.

The enthusiasts created a special lobbying organization: the *National Association for Year-Round School*. They used it to showcase the need for longer school calendars and special funding to pay for them (Cammarota, 1961; Springer, 2010; Smyth, 2013; United States Subcommittee on Elementary, Secondary, and Vocational Education, 1991).

Enthusiasts hoped that top politicians would support the extended school calendar. They cheered when President Obama stated that he would secure funding for it (Sisk & Siemaszko, 2010).

Journalists and economists questioned the president's pledge to get funding to extend the calendar. They doubted that he could muster enough congressional votes. They predicted that he would be forced to take away funds from other popular scholastic programs (Kneese & Ballinger, 2009).

Critics saw another problem with the extended school year: they detected few instances in which it had affected students' test scores. They concluded that it was forcing the students to suffer through weeks and sometimes months of boring and ineffective instruction (Corbin, 2009; Holland, 2009).

Critics stated that they would support the extended school year only if a key demand was met. They demanded the rehabilitation of ineffective teachers (Giordano, 2012b; Shields & Oberg, 2000).

The critics were impressed by the special lobbying association established to promote a longer school year. They decided to establish their own association. They came up with a catchy name for it: the Save Our Summers Alliance (Smyth, 2013).

EXAMINING SIMPLE SOLUTIONS

People looked for solutions to complex problems. They sometimes offered startlingly simple solutions.

Activity 10.1

Enthusiasts stated that fallout shelters would protect citizens from nuclear harm. How did groups respond?

Table 10.1 identifies two groups: politicians and members of the public.

Complete the table by indicating the ways in which groups responded to the enthusiasts. You can use symbols.

Use the symbol – if groups had low confidence in the enthusiasts. Use the symbol ± for moderate confidence and the symbol + for high confidence. As a final step, explain the bases for the symbols that you selected.

You can rely on the information in this chapter, additional information, or the information cited in the references. If you are reading this chapter with colleagues, you can confer with them.

Table 10.1. Enthusiasts Recommend Fallout Shelters

Groups	Response*	Explanation
Politicians		
Public		

*– Low
± Moderate
+ High

Activity 10.2

Enthusiasts stated that race-based school calendars would benefit students throughout the South. How did groups respond?

Table 10.2 identifies two groups: school administrators and parents.

Complete the table by indicating the ways in which groups responded to the enthusiasts. You can use symbols.

Use the symbol – if groups had low confidence in the enthusiasts. Use the symbol ± for moderate confidence and the symbol + for high confidence. As a final step, explain the bases for the symbols that you selected.

Table 10.2. Enthusiasts Recommend Race-Based School Calendars

Groups	Response*	Explanation
School Administrators		
Parents		

*– Low
± Moderate
+ High

Activity 10.3

Enthusiasts stated that longer school calendars would benefit students with disabilities. How did groups respond?

Table 10.3 identifies two groups: school administrators and parents.

Complete the table by indicating the ways in which groups responded to the enthusiasts. You can use symbols.

Use the symbol – if groups had low confidence in the enthusiasts. Use the symbol ± for moderate confidence and the symbol + for high confidence. As a final step, explain the bases for the symbols that you selected.

Table 10.3. Enthusiasts Recommend Extended School Calendars for Students with Disabilities

Groups	Response*	Explanation
School Administrators		
Parents		

*– Low
± Moderate
+ High

Activity 10.4

Enthusiasts stated that longer school calendars would benefit all students. How did groups respond?

Table 10.4 identifies two groups: school administrators and parents.

Complete the table by indicating the ways in which groups responded to the enthusiasts. You can use symbols.

Use the symbol – if groups had low confidence in the enthusiasts. Use the symbol ± for moderate confidence and the symbol + for high confidence. As a final step, explain the bases for the symbols that you selected.

Table 10.4. Enthusiasts Recommend Extended School Calendars for All Students

Groups	Response*	Explanation
School Administrators		
Parents		

*– Low
± Moderate
+ High

SUMMARY

People wished to find solutions for complex educational problems. They sometimes advocated remarkably simple solutions.

REFERENCES

Ackman goes to SEC in latest chapter of Herbalife saga. (2013, August 5). *CNBC.com*. Retrieved from http://www.cnbc.com/id/100938732.

Aggarwal, C. C. (2011). *Social network data analytics*. New York: Springer.

Ahmed-Ullah, N. S., & Secter, B. (2013, March 22). CPS to close 61 buildings, affecting 30,000 kids. *Chicago Tribune*. Retrieved from http://articles.chicagotribune.com/2013-03-22/news/ct-met-cps-school-closings-0322-20130322_1_school-buildings-elementary-schools-todd-babbitz.

Alamar, B. (2013). *Sports analytics: A guide for coaches, managers, and other decision makers*. New York: Columbia University Press.

Alamar, B., & Mehrotra, V. (2012, February 24). Beyond moneyball: The future of sports analytics. *Analytics-magazine.org*. Retrieved from http://www.analytics-magazine.org/special-articles/525-beyond-moneyball-the-future-of-sports-analytics.

Alexander, D. C. (1988). *Who's ruining our schools? The case against the NEA Teacher Union*. Washington, DC: Save Our Schools Research and Education Foundation.

Alexander, K. (2014, January 6). Texas education board reviews social studies textbooks. *Herald Democrat*. Retrieved from http://heralddemocrat.com/news/texas/texas-education-board-reviews-social-studies-textbooks.

Andersen, T., & Allen, E. (2012, December 2). Program to offer longer school days expanding in Massachusetts, four other states. *Boston Globe*. Retrieved from http://www.boston.com/news/local/massachusetts/2012/12/03/program

-offer-longer-school-days-expanding-massachusetts-four-other-states/mthpS5FK4UDxlIm8J9YD3J/story.html.

Angulo, E. (2013, August 25). To prevent school violence, teachers learn how to spot mental illness. *NBCNews.com*. Retrieved from http://dailynightly.nbcnews.com/_news/2013/08/25/16899570-to-prevent-school-violence-teachers-learn-how-to-spot-mental-illness.

Apartment approved as official fallout shelter. (1961). *Los Angeles Times*. Retrieved from http://pqasb.pqarchiver.com.

As governor, Mitch Daniels looked to censor academic writings and courses. (2013, July 16). *Indystar.com*. Retrieved from https://www.indystar.com/viewart/20130716/NEWS/307160061/As-governor-Mitch-Daniels-looked-censor-academic-writings-courses.

Austin Independent School District. (2011). *Austinisd.org*. Retrieved from http://www.austinisd.org/customer-service.

Bacal, R. (2011). *Perfect phrases for customer service: Hundreds of ready-to-use phrases for handling any customer service situation*. New York: McGraw-Hill.

Bai, M. (2005, July 17). The framing wars. *New York Times*. Retrieved from http://www.nytimes.com/2005/07/17/magazine/17DEMOCRATS.html.

Baker, A. (2012, August 10). Ex-CNN anchor joins debate vs. unions over teacher misconduct. *New York Times*. Retrieved from http://www.nytimes.com/2012/08/11/education/campbell-brown-joins-debate-over-teachers-unions.html.

Banchero, S. (2012, July 29). Tennessee directs Nashville to back charter school. *Wall Street Journal*. Retrieved from http://online.wsj.com/article/SB10000872396390444405804577557113369514618.html.

———. (2013, April 30). Learning goals spur backlash. *Wall Street Journal*. Retrieved from http://online.wsj.com/article/SB10001424127887323528404578455161694638692.html.

Banchero, S., & Campo-Flores, A. (2013, August 26). Biggest changes in a decade greet students. *Wall Street Journal*. Retrieved from http://online.wsj.com/article/SB10001424127887323980604579029303538525902.html.

Banchero, S., & Maher, K. (2013, September 10). Philadelphia schools reopen amid financial, academic distress. *Wall Street Journal*. Retrieved from http://online.wsj.com/article/SB10001424127887323864604579065461857093406.html.

Banchero, S., & Porter, C. (2013a, January 17). In pursuit of safety, schools' paths diverge. *Wall Street Journal*. Retrieved from http://online.wsj.com/article/SB10001424127887323783704578248113754373942.html.

REFERENCES

———. (2013b, March 22). Chicago moves to close 11% of elementary schools in fall. *Wall Street Journal*. Retrieved from http://online.wsj.com/article/SB10001424127887324373204578374882000603440.html.

Barack Obama complains about Fox News again. (2009, June 18). *FoxNews.com*. Retrieved from http://www.foxnews.com/story/0,2933,527141,00.html.

Barbaro, M. (2009, September 22). Mayor doesn't always live by his health rules. *New York Times*. Retrieved from http://www.nytimes.com/2009/09/23/dining/23bloom.html.

Barnes, B., & Barnes, B. (2014, January 28). HELP! The STAAR is coming! *Blueribbonnews.com*. Retrieved from http://blueribbonnews.com/2014/01/help-the-staar-is-coming-mathnasium-106.

Bebchuk, L. A., & Fried, J. M. (2004). *Pay without performance: The unfulfilled promise of executive compensation*. Cambridge, MA: Harvard University Press.

Bennett, D. A. (1992, June 12). We can rescue schools and turn a profit. *Baltimore Sun*. Retrieved from http://articles.baltimoresun.com/1992-06-12/news/1992164171_1_public-schools-school-system-school-district.

Bernard, S. (2009). Bailed-out banks bestow big bonuses. *Bankingmyway.com*. Retrieved from http://www.bankingmyway.com/save/report-bailed-out-banks-bestow-big-bonuses.

Bernat, R. (2012, December 28). A reluctant vote in favor of armed school guards. *Wall Street Journal*. Retrieved from http://online.wsj.com/article/SB10001424127887324669104578203353922899758.html.

Better approach to school discipline. (2014, June 13). *New York Times*. Retrieved from http://www.nytimes.com/2014/06/14/opinion/zero-tolerance-policies-need-to-be-tamed.html.

Bhasin, K. (2013, August 9). Shunning plus-size shoppers is key to Lululemon's strategy, insiders say. *Huffington Post*. Retrieved from http://www.huffingtonpost.com/2013/07/31/lululemon-plus-size_n_3675605.html.

Big bank execs: What they take home. (2007). *CNN.com*. Retrieved from http://money.cnn.com/news/specials/storysupplement/ceopay.

Birnbaum, M. (2010, March 18). Historians speak out against proposed Texas textbook changes. *Washington Post*. Retrieved from http://www.washingtonpost.com/wp-dyn/content/article/2010/03/17/AR2010031700560.html.

Blake, M. (2010, January/February). Revisionaries: How a group of Texas conservatives is rewriting your kids' textbooks. *Washington Monthly*. Retrieved from http://www.washingtonmonthly.com/features/2010/1001.blake.html.

Bloom, M. (2013, March 21). Some teachers want longer school year because they're now judged on how much students learn. *StateImpact Ohio*.

Retrieved from http://stateimpact.npr.org/ohio/2013/03/21/changes-to-ohio-teacher-evaluations-prompt-teachers-to-request-longer-school-year.

Bothmer, B. (2010). *Framing the sixties: The use and abuse of a decade from Ronald Reagan to George W. Bush.* Amherst: University of Massachusetts Press.

Bozell, L. B. (2013). *Collusion: How the media stole the 2012 election.* HarperCollins.

Bradburn, N. M., Sudman, S., & Wansink, B. (2004). *Asking questions: The definitive guide to questionnaire design for market research, political polls, and social and health questionnaires.* San Francisco: Jossey-Bass.

Brody, L. (2014, July 20). N.J. salary cap is driving away superintendents. *Wall Street Journal.* Retrieved from http://online.wsj.com/articles/n-j-salary-cap-is-driving-away-superintendents-1405906049.

Brooks, K. J. (2013a, September 5). Jacksonville man starts petition to change Forrest High School name. *Florida Times-Union.* Retrieved from http://jacksonville.com/news/metro/2013-09-05/story/jacksonville-man-starts-petition-change-forrest-high-school-name.

———. (2013b, September 17). Vitti says he, district ready to pursue charter students. *Florida Times-Union.* Retrieved from http://jacksonville.com/news/metro/2013-09-17/story/vitti-says-he-district-ready-pursue-charter-students.

———. (2013c, October 17). Common Core still moving ahead in Florida. *Florida Times-Union.* Retrieved from http://jacksonville.com/news/metro/2013-10-17/story/common-core-still-moving-ahead-florida.

Brown, C. (2012, July 29). Teachers unions go to bat for sexual predators. *Wall Street Journal.* Retrieved from http://online.wsj.com/article/SB10000872396390443437504577547313612049308.html.

Burns, G. (2005). *The moral veto: Framing contraception, abortion, and cultural pluralism in the United States.* Cambridge, UK: Cambridge University Press.

Cammarota, G. (1961). *Extending the school year.* Washington, DC: Association for Supervision and Curriculum Development.

Capps, E. (2011, February 8). Reining in school superintendent severance packages. *The Blog Land of Earl Capps.* Retrieved from http://earlcapps.blogspot.com/2011/02/reining-in-school-superintendent.html.

Carlson, L. T. (2013, October 12). Tea Party rallying against Common Core State Standards. *Wisconsin Rapids Tribune.* Retrieved from http://www.wisconsinrapidstribune.com/article/20131012/WRT/310120569.

Carr, S., & Gilbertson, A. (2013, February 1). Schools and for-profit managers don't mix, skeptics say. *NBCNews.com.* Retrieved from http://usnews.nbcnews.com/_news/2013/02/01/16797433-schools-and-for-profit-managers-dont-mix-skeptics-say.

REFERENCES

Center for Digital Education (2013, August 26). The time is right for big data and analytics in K–12 Education. Centerdigitaled.com. Retrieved from http://www.centerdigitaled.com/paper/The-Time-is-Right-for-Big-Data-and-Analytics-in-K-12-Education.html.

CEO gets cool $44M severance package for one day of work. (2012, July 7). *MSN.com*. Retrieved from http://now.msn.com.

CEOs with severance packages underperform by up to 4%. (2011, December 7). *ChiefExecutive.net*. Retrieved from http://chiefexecutive.net/ceos-with-severance-packages-underperform-by-4.

Chapman, M. (2013, January 10). Herbalife defends itself against Ackman's claims. *AP News*. Retrieved from http://bigstory.ap.org/article/herbalife-defends-itself-against-ackmans-claims.

Chenoweth, K. (2012, February, 3). Principals matter: School leaders can drive student learning. *Huffington Post*. Retrieved from http://www.huffingtonpost.com/Karin%20Chenoweth/principals-matter-school-_b_1252598.html.

Chicago kids crossing gang boundaries escorted to school. (2013, August 26). *USA TODAY*. Retrieved from http://www.usatoday.com/story/news/nation/2013/08/26/chicago-schools-violence/2700373.

Childs, R. (2011, January 6). A Bizarro World where teachers are to blame. *Socialistworker.org*. Retrieved from http://socialistworker.org/2011/01/06/anti-teacher-bizarro-world.

Chung, J. (2013a, January 9). Showdown over Herbalife spotlights new Wall Street. *Wall Street Journal*. Retrieved from http://online.wsj.com/article/SB10001424127887324081704578231522781739266.html.

———. (2013b, March 31). In Herbalife fight, both sides prevail. *Wall Street Journal*. Retrieved from http://online.wsj.com/news/articles/SB10001424127887323361804578388682197247250.

Churney, D. (2008, September 8). Fallout fever: Civil Defense shelters dotted area cities during the Cold War. *My Web Times*. Retrieved from http://mywebtimes.com/archives/ottawa/display.php?id=366305.

Clayton, S. (2012, May 2). Philadelphia inspires PA bill capping superintendent severance packages. *Philadelphia Public Policy Examiner*. Retrieved from http://www.examiner.com/article/philadelphia-inspires-pa-bill-capping-superintendent-severance-packages.

Clifford, S. (2013, March 21). Recall is expensive setback for maker of yoga pants. *New York Times*. Retrieved from http://www.nytimes.com/2013/03/22/business/lululemon-says-yoga-pants-mishap-will-be-costly.html.

Cohn, N. (2013, January 14). Has Nate Silver forever changed statistics? *New Republic*. Retrieved from http://www.newrepublic.com/book/review/has-nate-silver-forever-changed-statistics.

Collins, G. (2012, April 27). A very pricey pineapple. *New York Times*. Retrieved from http://www.nytimes.com/2012/04/28/opinion/collins-a-very-pricey-pineapple.html.

Company overview of Florida Virtual School. (2013, September 11). *Businessweek*. Retrieved from http://investing.businessweek.com/research/stocks/private/snapshot.asp?privcapId=34819569.

Connor, T. (2013, August 8). Bulletproof school supplies get low grades from safety experts. *NBCNews.com*. Retrieved from http://usnews.nbcnews.com/_news/2013/08/21/20107023-bulletproof-school-supplies-get-low-grades-from-safety-experts.

Cook, C., & Moore, T. (2013, March 8). Doing a Texas two-step around education reform. *Wall Street Journal*. Retrieved from http://online.wsj.com/article/SB10001424127887324081704578233814190553202.html.

Corbin, C. (2009, September 29). Extended school year would have dire economic effects, critics say. *FoxNews.com*. Retrieved from http://www.foxnews.com/politics/2009/09/29/extended-school-year-dire-economic-effects-critics-say.

Cramer, P. (2012, February 15). More than $5 million in bonuses given to leaders at 275 schools. *Chalkbeat New York*. Retrieved from http://gothamschools.org/2012/02/15/more-than-5-million-in-bonuses-given-to-leaders-at-275-schools.

Curriden, M. (2012, June 1). The lawyers of Watergate: How a "3rd-rate burglary" provoked new standards for lawyer ethics. *ABA Journal*. Retrieved from http://www.abajournal.com/magazine/article/the_lawyers_of_watergate_how_a_3rd-rate_burglary_provoked_new_standards.

Curtis, D. (2012, April). How I beat a patent troll [video]. *TED*. Retrieved from http://www.ted.com/talks/drew_curtis_how_i_beat_a_patent_troll.html.

Daily poll: Should principals and teachers be armed? (2012, December 20). *Jersey Journal*. Retrieved from http://www.nj.com/hudson/voices/index.ssf/2012/12/daily_poll_should_principals_a_1.html#/0.

Darling-Hammond, L. (2012, June 24). No: Teaching is too complex. *Wall Street Journal*. Retrieved from http://online.wsj.com/article/SB10001424052702304723304577366023832205042.html.

Dash, E. (2011, September 29). Outsize severance continues for executives, even after failed tenures. *New York Times*. Retrieved from http://www.nytimes.com/2011/09/30/business/outsize-severance-continues-for-executives-even-after-failed-tenures.html.

Davenport, T. H., & Harris, J. G. (2007). *Competing on analytics: The new science of winning*. Boston: Harvard Business School Press.

REFERENCES

Davey, M. (2013, August 26). In Chicago, campaign to provide safe passage on way to school. *New York Times.* Retrieved from http://www.nytimes.com/2013/08/27/education/in-chicago-campaign-to-provide-safe-passage-on-way-to-school.html.

Davey, M., & Greenhouse, S. (2012, September 3). Ohio unions battle conservative super PACS for votes. *New York Times.* Retrieved from http://www.nytimes.com/2012/09/04/us/politics/ohio-unions-face-tough-battle-with-super-pacs.html.

Dawson, C. (2012, October 10). Are big data approaches the answer to K12 educational pain points? *ZDNet Education.* Retrieved from http://www.zdnet.com/are-big-data-approaches-the-answer-to-k12-educational-pain-points-7000005297.

Dean, J. W., & Robenalt, J. (2012, Spring). The legacy of Watergate. *Litigation.* Retrieved from http://www.americanbar.org/publications/litigation_journal/2011_12/spring/watergate_legacy.html.

Dear Bill and Melinda: "These are not rhetorical questions. I would really like answers." (2013, June 15). *Teachers' Letters to Bill Gates.* Retrieved from http://teacherslettersobillgates.com/2013/06/15/dear-bill-and-melinda-these-are-not-rhetorical-questions-i-would-really-like-answers-norma.

DeLapp, T. (2007). Public school customer relations. *Communication Resources for Schools.* Retrieved from http://www.tomdelapp.com/workshops_customer_relations.html.

Delisio, E. (2009, February 24). Schools offering service with a smile. *Education World.* Retrieved from http://www.educationworld.com/a_admin/admin/admin430.shtml.

Delta one of top airlines to get an "F" in report. (2009, March 11). *CNN.com.* Retrieved from http://www.cnn.com/2009/TRAVEL/03/11/airlines.report.card/index.html.

Delta tops 2013 FORTUNE world's most admired companies airline industry list. (2013, February 28). *Delta Air Lines.* Retrieved from http://news.delta.com/index.php?s=43&item=1904.

DeMarche, E. (2013, September 18). Second Amendment definition in Texas school work book triggers uproar. *FoxNews.com.* Retrieved from http://www.foxnews.com/us/2013/09/18/texas-high-school-work-book-stirs-controversy-over-edited-definition-second.

Dick Morris to Piers Morgan on Fox News firing: "I was wrong at the top of my lungs" [Video]. (2013, February 7). *Huffington Post.* Retrieved from http://www.huffingtonpost.com/2013/02/07/dick-morris-piers-morgan-i-was-wrong-fox-news_n_2637464.html.

Dillon, S. (2011, February 7). U.S. plan to replace principals hits snag: Who will step in? *New York Times.* Retrieved from http://www.nytimes.com/2011/02/08/education/08education.html.

Dixon, M. (2013, October 16). State education board rejects mandatory use of certain Common Core materials. *Florida Times-Union.* Retrieved from http://jacksonville.com/news/2013-10-15/story/state-education-board-rejects-mandatory-use-certain-common-core-materials.

Dlott, S. (2007). *Surviving and thriving as a superintendent of schools: Leadership lessons from modern American presidents.* Lanham, MD: Rowman & Littlefield.

DuFour, R., & Mattos, M. (2013, April). How do principals really improve schools? *Principalship.* Retrieved from http://www.ascd.org/publications/educational-leadership/apr13/vol70/num07/How-Do-Principals-Really-Improve-Schools%C2%A2.aspx.

Duval County Public Schools. (2010). Duval virtual instruction academy. *Duvalschools.org.* Retrieved from http://www.duvalschools.org/dvia.

Dwyer, J. (2013, August 16). The impossible mayor of the possible. *New York Times.* Retrieved from http://www.nytimes.com/2013/08/18/nyregion/the-impossible-mayor-of-the-possible.html.

EdisonLearning, Inc. (2013). *Insideview.com.* Retrieved from http://www.insideview.com/directory/edisonlearning-inc.

Education analytics for K–12. (2013). *Microsoft.com.* Retrieved from http://www.microsoft.com/education/en-us/solutions/Pages/education_analytics.aspx.

Edwards, J. A., & Weiss, D. (Eds.). (2011). *The rhetoric of American Exceptionalism: Critical essays.* Jefferson, NC: McFarland.

Eligon, J. (2013, April 14). A Missouri school trains its teachers to carry guns, and most parents approve. *New York Times.* Retrieved from http://www.nytimes.com/2013/04/15/us/missouri-school-trains-teachers-to-carry-guns.html.

Elsberg, T. (1988, February 8). Don't take away tenure of school principals. *New York Times.* Retrieved from http://www.nytimes.com/1988/02/08/opinion/l-don-t-take-away-tenure-of-school-principals-870788.html.

End of exorbitant CEO exit packages?—Don't hold your breath. (2012, July 18). *Knowledge@Wharton.* Retrieved from http://knowledge.wharton.upenn.edu/article.cfm?articleid=3052.

Ending tenure for principals. (1999, November 30). *New York Times.* Retrieved from http://www.nytimes.com/1999/11/30/opinion/ending-tenure-for-principals.html.

Entman, R. M. (2003). *Projections of power: Framing news, public opinion, and U.S. foreign policy.* Chicago: University of Chicago Press.

REFERENCES

Everything you need to know about charter schools. (2013, August 1). *StateImpact Florida*. Retrieved from http://stateimpact.npr.org/florida/tag/charter-schools.

Executive pay. (2012, October 10). *New York Times*. Retrieved from http://topics.nytimes.com/top/reference/timestopics/subjects/e/executive_pay/index.html.

Farah, S. (2013, February 19). Texas lawmaker gives standardized tests the boot. *CollegXpress.com*. Retrieved from http://www.collegexpress.com/counselors-and-parents/college-counselors/blog/texas-lawmaker-gives-standardized-tests-boot.

Fausset, R. (2014, August 10). In Atlanta, jury selection is set to begin in test scandal. *New York Times*. Retrieved from http://www.nytimes.com/2014/08/11/us/atlanta-jury-selection-set-to-begin-school-employees-accused-of-altering-test-scores.html.

Fawcett, M. (2013, June 14). "Patent trolls" destroy value and innovation—Am I dreaming? *Forbes.com*. Retrieved from http://www.forbes.com/sites/netapp/2013/06/14/patent-trolls-pae.

Feldman, R. (2012). *Rethinking patent law*. Cambridge, MA: Harvard University Press.

Feulner, E. J. (2014). A national GPS device. *Heritage.org*. Retrieved from http://www.heritage.org/research/commentary/2014/8/a-national-gps-device.

Fisher, M. (2012, June 14). Watergate: The long shadow of a scandal. *Washington Post*. Retrieved from http://www.washingtonpost.com/lifestyle/style/latest-headlines/2010/08/25/gJQAKVYcdV_story.html.

Flaccus, G. (2013, January 1). School brings in high-powered assault weapons. *NBCNews.com*. Retrieved from http://usnews.nbcnews.com/_news/2013/01/24/16677346-school-brings-in-high-powered-assault-weapons.

Flannery, N. P. (2012, January 19). Executive compensation: The true cost of the 10 largest CEO severance packages of the past decade. *Forbes*. Retrieved from http://www.forbes.com/sites/nathanielparishflannery/2012/01/19/billion-dollar-blowout-top-10-largest-ceo-severance-packages-of-the-past-decade.

Fleisher. L. (2013, June 3). Teacher plan uncertain. *Wall Street Journal*. Retrieved from http://online.wsj.com/article/SB10001424127887324563004578521893604212284.html.

Florida Virtual School employer reviews. (2013). *Indeed.com*. Retrieved from http://www.indeed.com/cmp/Florida-Virtual-School/reviews.

Florida Virtual School reviews. (2013). *Glassdoor.com*. Retrieved from http://www.glassdoor.com/Reviews/Florida-Virtual-School-Reviews-E34128.htm.

Florida's shameful situation on charter schools. (2012, October 30). *Bradenton Herald*. Retrieved from http://www.bradenton.com/2012/10/30/4257940/florida-shameful-situation-on.html.

Focus on the real issue at Forrest High School, the students. (2013, September 20). *Florida Times-Union*. Retrieved from http://members.jacksonville.com/opinion/premium-opinion/2013-09-20/story/focus-real-issue-forrest-high-school-students.

Foster, P. (2012, December 28). Teachers flocked to a free gun training course after the Newtown massacre. *BusinessInsider.com*. Retrieved from http://www.businessinsider.com/utah-teachers-flocked-to-gun-training-2012-12.

Freeland, R. F. (2001). *The struggle for control of the modern corporation: Organizational change at General Motors, 1924–1970*. Cambridge, UK: Cambridge University Press.

Friedman, S. (2013, April 4). $90 million tab for STAAR testing includes pricey meetings, travel, consultants. *NBCDFW.com*. Retrieved from http://www.nbcdfw.com/investigations/90-Million-Tab-for-STAAR-Testing-Includes-Pricey-Meetings-Travel-Consultants-201520411.html.

Fuchs, E. (2013, June 15). This man is either the world's biggest patent troll or a champion of innovation. *Seattlepi.com*. Retrieved from http://www.seattlepi.com/technology/businessinsider/article/This-Man-Is-Either-The-World-s-Biggest-Patent-4593254.php.

Gillers, S. (2012, June 13). The bar got tough on ethics. *New York Times*. Retrieved from http://www.nytimes.com/roomfordebate/2012/06/13/did-any-good-come-of-watergate/one-lasting-change-bar-associations-ethics-rules.

Gingrich, N., & Haley, V. (2011). *A nation like no other: Why American Exceptionalism matters*. Washington, DC: Regnery.

Giordano, G. (2000). *Twentieth-century reading education: Understanding practices of today in terms of patterns of the past*. London, UK: Elsevier/JAI.

———. (2003). *Twentieth-century textbook wars: A history of advocacy and opposition*. New York: Peter Lang.

———. (2004). *Wartime schools: How World War II changed American education*. New York: Peter Lang.

———. (2005). *How testing came to dominate American schools: The history of educational assessment*. New York: Peter Lang.

———. (2007). *American special education: A history of early political advocacy*. New York: Peter Lang.

———. (2009). *Solving education's problems effectively: A guide to using the case method*. Lanham, MD: Rowman & Littlefield.

———. (2010). *Cockeyed education: A case method primer*. Lanham, MD: Rowman & Littlefield.

REFERENCES

———. (2011). *Lopsided schools: Case method briefings*. Lanham, MD: Rowman & Littlefield.

———. (2012a). *Capping costs: Putting a price tag on school reform*. Lanham, MD: Rowman & Littlefield.

———. (2012b). *Teachers go to rehab: Historical and current advice to instructors*. Lanham, MD: Rowman & Littlefield.

———. (2014). *Commonsense questions about instruction: The answers can provide essential steps to improvement*. Lanham, MD: Rowman & Littlefield.

Girdner, R. (2012, May 21). Florida Virtual School: Is it the future of education in Florida? *Ecorsair.com*. Retrieved from http://ecorsair.com/?p=7383.

Goldberg, B. (2001). *Bias: A CBS insider exposes how the media distort the news*. Washington, DC: Regnery.

Gonzalez, S. (2012, August 28). How students take physical education online. *StateImpact Florida*. Retrieved from http://stateimpact.npr.org/florida/2012/08/28/how-students-take-physical-education-online.

Goode, E. (2013, March 14). Focusing on violence before it happens. *New York Times*. Retrieved from http://www.nytimes.com/2013/03/15/us/in-los-angeles-focusing-on-violence-before-it-occurs.html.

Gootmans, E. (2004, March 31). Recruiting 40 principals for city schools, and offering signing bonuses to some, too. *New York Times*. Retrieved from http://www.nytimes.com/2004/03/31/nyregion/recruiting-40-principals-for-city-schools-offering-signing-bonuses-some-too.html.

Graham, A. (2001). *Framing the South: Hollywood, television, and race during the Civil Rights struggle*. Baltimore: Johns Hopkins University Press.

Graham, M. D., Roth, T. A., & Dugan, D. (2008). *Effective executive compensation: Creating a total rewards strategy for executives*. New York: AMACOM.

Harris, C. (2013, October 9). TISD meets all four STAAR test score requirements. *Tribunenews.com*. Retrieved from http://www.tribunenews.com/index.php/k2/edition-categories/local-news/item/1157-tisd-meets-all-four-staar-test-score-requirements.

Hartocollis, A. (2001, May 26). Levy to award merit bonuses to principals. *New York Times*. Retrieved from http://www.nytimes.com/2001/05/26/nyregion/levy-to-award-merit-bonuses-to-principals.html.

Hastings, D. (2013, September 13). Florida school named after KKK leader won't change name despite petition, longstanding protests. *New York Daily News*. Retrieved from http://www.nydailynews.com/news/national/thousands-florida-school-drop-kkk-leader-article-1.1455200.

Henderson, R. D., Urban, W. J., & Wolman, P. (2004). *Teacher unions and education policy: Retrenchment or reform?* Amsterdam: Elsevier.

Hernández, J. C. (2014, May 11). Charters, public schools and a chasm between. *New York Times.* Retrieved from http://www.nytimes.com/2014/05/12/ny region/charters-public-schools-and-a-chasm-between.htm.

Hiaasen, S., & McGrory, K. (2011, December 10). Florida charter schools: Big money, little oversight. *Miami Herald.* Retrieved from http://www.miamiherald.com/2011/09/19/v-fullstory/2541051/florida-charter-schools-big-money.html.

Hibberd, N. (2013, February 18). Texas the most taxing testing state for students. *MyFoxHouston.com.* Retrieved from http://www.myfoxhouston.com/story/21237224/2013/02/18/texas-the-testiest-state-for-students.

Hidden in plain view. (2000, June 6). *Kilroywashere.org.* Retrieved from http://www.kilroywashere.org/006-Pages/Bunker.html.

Highly effective principals raise student achievement: Study posted. (2012, October 24). *Huffington Post.* Retrieved from http://www.huffingtonpost.com/2012/10/24/highly-effective-principa_n_2009816.html.

Hiltzik, M. (2013, June 7). White House trying to clear the forest of "patent trolls." *Los Angeles Times.* Retrieved from http://articles.latimes.com/2013/jun/07/business/la-fi-hiltzik-20130609.

Hirshleifer, J., & Riley, J. G. (1992). *The analytics of uncertainty and information.* Cambridge, UK: Cambridge University Press.

Hodges, D. (2013, August). How your child is being dumbed down. *Thecommonsenseshow.com.* Retrieved from http://www.thecommonsenseshow.com/2013/08/02/how-your-child-is-being-dumbed-down.

Hodgson, G. (2009). *The myth of American Exceptionalism.* New Haven, CT: Yale University Press.

Holland, S. (2009, September 4). Despite push, year-round schools get mixed grades. *CNN.com.* Retrieved from http://articles.cnn.com/2009-09-04/us/us.year.round.schools_1_school-year-school-day-school-week?_s=PM:US.

Horn, M. (2013, August 1). For-profits: Aid or vice in public education? *Forbes.* Retrieved from http://www.forbes.com/sites/michaelhorn/2013/08/01/for-profits-aid-or-vice-in-public-education.

Huang, T. (2011, March 2). Framing stories. *Poynter.org.* Retrieved from http://www.poynter.org/how-tos/newsgathering-storytelling/diversity-at-work/47657/framing-stories.

Hurdle, J. (2012, December 30). Struggling district in Philadelphia plans to close 37 schools. *New York Times.* Retrieved from http://www.nytimes.com/2012/12/31/education/philadelphia-district-may-close-37-schools.html.

———. (2013, March 7). Philadelphia officials vote to close 23 schools. *New York Times.* Retrieved from http://www.nytimes.com/2013/03/08/education/philadelphia-officials-vote-to-close-23-schools.html.

REFERENCES

Ignatieff, M. (Ed.). (2005). *American Exceptionalism and human rights*. Princeton, NJ: Princeton University Press.

In Georgia, schools learn from Ritz-Carlton to roll out the red carpet for students' families. (2013, September 8). *Washington Post*. Retrieved from http://www.washingtonpost.com/national/in-georgia-schools-learn-from-ritz-carlton-to-roll-out-the-red-carpet-for-students-families/2013/09/08/f437b6d2-1893-11e3-80ac-96205cacb45a_story.html.

It's time to change name of Forrest High School. (2013, October 18). *Florida Times-Union*. Retrieved from http://members.jacksonville.com/opinion/premium-opinion/2013-10-18/story/its-time-change-name-forrest-high-school.

Jenkins, H. W. (2013, February 19). Let Herbalife customers decide. *Wall Street Journal*. Retrieved from http://online.wsj.com/article/SB10001424127887323495104578313980860182920.html.

Jerry Brown's school bailout. (2012, October 2). *Wall Street Journal*. Retrieved from http://online.wsj.com/article/SB10000872396390444180004578016673576896076.html.

John Liu on education policy. (2013). *Chalkbeat New York*. Retrieved from http://gothamschools.org/2013-mayoral-race.

Johnson, C. C., & Thomas, G. (2013, April 12). What caused the Bowdoin College diversity dustup? [Video]. *Dailycaller.com*. Retrieved from http://dailycaller.com/2013/05/12/what-caused-the-bowdoin-college-diversity-dustup-video.

Johnson, K. (2013, February 18). Authorities' new advice to schools: Confront shooter. *USA TODAY*. Retrieved from http://www.usatoday.com/story/news/nation/2013/02/18/schools-advice-confront-shooters/1920601.

Johnson-Cartee, K. S. (2005). *News narratives and news framing: Constructing political reality*. Lanham, MD: Rowman & Littlefield.

Jordan, G. (2013, March 15). House Republicans and Democrats spar over charter school bias charge. *StateImpact Florida*. Retrieved from http://stateimpact.npr.org/florida/2013/03/15/house-republicans-and-democrats-spar-over-charter-school-bias-charge.

Kain, E. (2011, September 29). 80% of Michigan charter schools are for-profits. *Forbes.com*. Retrieved from http://www.forbes.com/sites/erikkain/2011/09/29/80-of-michigan-charter-schools-are-for-profits.

Kamenetz, A. (2014, August 17). Why the Atlanta testing scandal matters. *NprEd*. Retrieved from http://www.npr.org/blogs/ed/2014/08/17/340412133/why-the-atlanta-testing-scandal-matters.

Kamin, M. (2006). *Customer service training*. Oxford, UK: Pergamon.

Kendall, D. E. (2005). *Framing class: Media representations of wealth and poverty in America*. Lanham, MD: Rowman & Littlefield.

Kenney, C. (2011, December 16). Why airlines keep going bankrupt. *Planet Money*. Retrieved from http://www.npr.org/blogs/money/2011/12/16/143765367/why-airlines-keep-going-bankrupt.

Kenny, D. (2012, June 24). Why charter schools work. *Wall Street Journal*. Retrieved from http://online.wsj.com/article/SB10001424052702303703004577472422188140892.html.

Kieff, F. S., & Paredes, T. (Eds.). (2012). *Perspectives on commercializing innovation*. Cambridge, UK: Cambridge University Press.

Kingsbury, A. (2012, September 19). Outgoing Rochester school superintendent could get $181,000 severance. *Oakland Press*. Retrieved from http://www.theoaklandpress.com/articles/2012/09/19/news/local_news/doc5059abc61e7fd825978144.txt.

Kirpaug, D. L. (2014, August 16). Teaching is not a business. *New York Times*. Retrieved from http://www.nytimes.com/2014/08/17/opinion/sunday/teaching-is-not-a-business.html.

Klein, P. (2007, September). Are large CEO severance packages justified? *KelloggInsight*. Retrieved from http://insight.kellogg.northwestern.edu/index.php/Kellogg/article/are_large_ceo_severance_packages_justified.

Klein, R. (2013, September 9). Texas textbook hearing incites debate over whether students should learn creationism. *Huffington Post*. Retrieved from http://www.huffingtonpost.com/2013/09/18/texas-textbook-hearings_n_3949676.html.

Kleinz, K. H. (2013). Sensational customer service—Savvy schools finding ways to make it work. *National School Public Relations Association*. Retrieved from http://www.nspra.org/professional_communicators.

Kneese, C., & Ballinger, C. E. (Eds.). (2009). *Balancing the school calendar: Perspectives from the public and stakeholders*. Lanham, MD: Rowman & Littlefield.

Koshik, I. (2005). *Beyond rhetorical questions: Assertive questions in everyday interaction*. Amsterdam: Benjamins.

Kowalski, T. J. (2000). *Public relations in schools*. Upper Saddle River, NJ: Merrill.

———. (2010). *The school principal: Visionary leadership and competent management*. New York: Routledge.

Kravitz, D. (2013, November 18). Is New York's charter-school era waning? *New Yorker*. Retrieved from http://www.newyorker.com/online/blogs/currency/2013/11/is-new-yorks-charter-school-era-waning.html.

Kubrick, S. [director]. (2001). *Dr. Strangelove: Or, how I learned to stop worrying and love the bomb* [Film]. Burbank, CA: Columbia.

REFERENCES

La Roche, J. (2012, December 2). We have never seen anything like Bill Ackman's dizzying takedown of Herbalife. *BusinessInsider.com*. Retrieved from http://www.businessinsider.com/bill-ackmans-herbalife-presentation-2012-12.

Ladd, J. M. (2012). *Why Americans hate the media and how it matters*. Princeton, NJ: Princeton University Press.

Lederman, J. (2012, December 2). Class time increases in 5 states in effort to improve U.S. public education. *Huffington Post*. Retrieved from http://www.huffingtonpost.com/2012/12/02/class-time-increases-in-5_n_2229411.html.

Lewis, M. (2003). *Moneyball: The art of winning an unfair game*. New York: Norton.

Lichtblau, E. (2013, January 11). Makers of violent video games marshal support to fend off regulation. *New York Times*. Retrieved from http://www.nytimes.com/2013/01/12/us/politics/makers-of-violent-video-games-marshal-support-to-fend-off-regulation.html.

Liebman, J. (2012, August 27). The Delta customer service nightmare that made my mother miss her brother's funeral. *BusinessInsider.com*. Retrieved from http://www.businessinsider.com/the-delta-customer-service-nightmare-that-made-my-mother-miss-her-brothers-funeral-2012-8.

Liebowitz, J. (2013, June 6). Smart analytics in education. *SAS.com*. Retrieved from http://www.sas.com/knowledge-exchange/business-analytics/innovation/smart-analytics-in-education/index.html.

Lipman, F. D., & Hall, S. E. (2008). *Executive compensation best practices*. Hoboken, NJ: Wiley.

Loeb, S., & Grissom, J. A. (2013, July 9). What do we know about the use of value-added measures for principal evaluation? *Carnegieknowledgenetwork.org*. Retrieved from http://www.carnegieknowledgenetwork.org/briefs/value-added/principal-evaluation.

Lopez, A. (2013, August 7). Virtual schools are spending millions of taxpayer dollars on advertising. *Florida Center for Investigative Reporting*. Retrieved from http://fcir.org/2013/08/07/k12-inc-florida-for-profit-schools.

Loveless, T. (2000). *Conflicting missions? Teachers unions and educational reform*. Washington, DC: Brookings Institution Press.

Mack, S. (2013, October 1). Not just Florida's problem: New York City charter schools have fewer children with disabilities. *State Impact Florida*. Retrieved from http://stateimpact.npr.org/florida/2013/10/01/not-just-floridas-problem-new-york-city-charter-schools-have-fewer-children-with-disabilities.

Madhani, A. (2013, September 24). Obama tells the world: America is exceptional. *USA TODAY*. Retrieved from http://www.usatoday.com/story/news/world/2013/09/24/obama-america-exceptionalism-putin-un/2861129.

Mahler, J. (2011, April 9). The deadlocked debate over education reform. *New York Times*. Retrieved from http://www.nytimes.com/2011/04/10/weekinreview/10reform.html.

Marcus, G., & Davis, E. (2013, January 25). What Nate Silver gets wrong. *New Yorker*. Retrieved from http://www.newyorker.com/online/blogs/books/2013/01/what-nate-silver-gets-wrong.html.

Margo, R. A. (1990). *Race and schooling in the South, 1880–1950: An economic history*. Chicago: University of Chicago Press.

Maryland police to review arrest of parent who objected to Common Core. (2013, September 23). *FoxNews.com*. Retrieved from http://www.foxnews.com/us/2013/09/23/maryland-police-to-review-arrest-parent-who-objected-to-common-core.

Matsuura, J. H. (2008). *Jefferson vs. the patent trolls: A populist vision of intellectual property rights*. Charlottesville: University of Virginia Press.

Matthews, C. (2013, June 14). No, the Lululemon CEO didn't get fired for see-through yoga pants. *Time: Business*. Retrieved from http://business.time.com/2013/06/14/no-the-lululemon-ceo-didnt-get-fired-for-see-through-yoga-pants.

Mattioli, D. (2012, March 22). Lululemon's secret sauce. *Wall Street Journal*. Retrieved from http://online.wsj.com/article/SB10001424052702303812904577295882632723066.html.

Mayor's education legacy an issue in NYC race. (2013, June 2). *Wall Street Journal*. Retrieved from http://online.wsj.com/article/APfbbf75639925415eb5549eeeebae3a25.html.

McAdoo, M. (2013, July 3). U.S. Teachers paid less, work longer, than OECD average. *Edwize.org*. Retrieved from http://www.edwize.org.

McCartney, S. (2011, February 3). Delta sends its 11,000 agents to charm school. *Wall Street Journal*. Retrieved from http://online.wsj.com/news/articles/SB10001424052748704775604576120080627254652.

McConnell, M. (2012, February 27). Should parents have the power to pull the trigger on schools? *Deseret News*. Retrieved from http://educatingourselves.blogs.deseretnews.com/2012/02/27/should-parents-have-the-power-to-pull-the-trigger-on-schools.

McGrory, K. (2013, May 13). Bill opens up funding for private virtual schools. *Tampa Bay Times*. Retrieved from http://www.tampabay.com/news/education/k12/bill-opens-up-funding-for-private-virtual-schools/2120631.

McWilliams, J. (2011, June 21). Delta gets airlines' lowest customer satisfaction score. *Atlanta Journal Constitution*. Retrieved from http://www.ajc.com/news/business/delta-gets-airlines-lowest-customer-satisfaction-s/nQwbw.

REFERENCES

Middleton, K. E., & Petitt, E. A. (2007). *Who cares? Improving public schools through relationships and customer service*. Tucson, AZ: Wheatmark.

Miller, B., De, L. M., Horovitz, R., Pitt, B., Rudin, S., Karsch, A., & Kimmel, S. (2012). *Moneyball* [Film]. Culver City, CA: Sony.

Miller, L. S. (1995). *An American imperative: Accelerating minority educational advancement*. New Haven, CT: Yale University Press.

Mintzberg, H. (2012, June 14). No more executive bonuses! *Wall Street Journal*. Retrieved from http://online.wsj.com/article/SB10001424052748703294 00457451122349453657O.html.

Mitchell, M. N. (2010). *Raising freedom's child: Black children and visions of the future after slavery*. New York: New York University Press.

Monteyne, D. (2011). *Fallout shelter: Designing for civil defense in the Cold War*. Minneapolis: University of Minnesota Press.

Mooney, A. (2010, September 28). Obama: Fox News is "destructive" to America. *CNN.com*. Retrieved from http://politicalticker.blogs.cnn.com/2010/09/28/obama-fox-news-is-destructive-to-america.

Moore, E. H. (2009). *School public relations for student success*. Thousand Oaks, CA: Corwin.

Morey, P., & Yaqin, A. (2011). *Framing Muslims: Stereotyping and representation after 9/11*. Cambridge, MA: Harvard University Press.

Mullins, J. W. (2006). *The new business road test: What entrepreneurs and executives should do before writing a business plan*. Harlow, UK: Prentice Hall.

National School Public Relations Association (2013). Our mission. *Nspra.org*. Retrieved from http://www.nspra.org/our_mission.

Nelson, B. S., & Sassi, A. (2005). *The effective principal: Instructional leadership for high-quality learning*. New York: Teachers College Press.

New York City public school parents. (2013, April 27). Why do the media nearly always frame education issues as the UFT vs. the Mayor. *Author*. Retrieved from http://nycpublicschoolparents.blogspot.com/2013/04/why-does-media-nearly-always-frame.html.

No choice: Students with disabilities and Florida's charter schools. (2013). *StateImpact Florida*. Retrieved from http://stateimpact.npr.org/florida/tag/disabled-in-florida-charters.

Norlin, J. W. (2008). *Extended school year services under the IDEA and Section 504: Legal standards and case law*. Horsham, PA: LRP.

Noveck, J. (2012, November 11). Election, statistician finds celebrity. *Huffington Post*. Retrieved from http://www.huffingtonpost.com/2012/11/09/nate-silver-celebrity_n_2103761.html.

Obama: Republicans too "worried about what Rush Limbaugh is going to say." (2013, August 23). *Huffington Post*. Retrieved from http://www.huffington post.com/2013/08/23/obama-republicans-rush-limbaugh_n_3803680.html.

O'Connor, J. (2012, September 11). Florida investigates K12, nation's largest online educator. *StateImpact Florida*. Retrieved from http://stateimpact.npr.org/florida/2012/09/11/florida-investigates-k12-nations-largest-online-educator.

———. (2013, August 1). A look at the Indiana charter school at the center of Tony Bennett's resignation. *StateImpact Florida*. Retrieved from http://stateimpact.npr.org/florida/2013/08/01/a-look-at-the-indiana-charter-school-at-the-center-of-tony-bennetts-resignation.

O'Donnell, P. (2012, September 30). Online schools get millions in public support. *Plain Dealer*. Retrieved from http://www.cleveland.com/metro/index.ssf/2012/09/online_schools_get_millions_in.html.

Page, S. (2014, August 12). Once allies, now in conflict: Teachers union and Obama. *USA TODAY*. Retrieved from http://www.usatoday.com/story/news/politics/2014/08/12/capital-download-nea-president-on-friction-with-obama/13941101.

Patten, D. (2013, February 6). Dick Morris says Fox News fired him "for being wrong." *Deadline.com*. Retrieved from http://www.deadline.com/2013/02/dick-morris-dropped-by-fox-news.

Petition targets Fla. school named for KKK leader. (2013, September 25). *USA TODAY*. Retrieved from http://www.usatoday.com/story/news/nation/2013/09/25/jacksonville-kkk-school-name-petition/2872953.

Philbin, B. (2013, February 26). Wall Street's cash bonus pool hits $20 billion. *Wall Street Journal*. Retrieved from http://online.wsj.com/article/SB10001424127887324338604578328163550389242.html.

Phillips, A. M. (2012, February 15). City gives $5.7 million to principals in bonuses. *Schoolbook.org*. Retrieved from http://www.schoolbook.org/2012/02/15/city-gives-nearly-6-million-to-principals-in-bonuses.

Picciano, A. G., & Spring, J. H. (2013). *The great American education-industrial complex: Ideology, technology, and profit*. New York: Routledge.

Piette, B. (2013, October 11). Philadelphia: Our schools are not for sale! *Workers World*. Retrieved from http://www.workers.org/articles/2013/10/11/philadelphia-schools-sale.

Porter, C. (2013, May 1). Charter schools unionize. *Wall Street Journal*. Retrieved from http://online.wsj.com/article/SB10001424127887324582004578457301633830668.html.

———. (2014, August 26). Schools welcome guards, fences—and students. *Wall Street Journal*. Retrieved from http://online.wsj.com/articles/new-safety-measures-greet-students-1408990492.

REFERENCES

Principles. (2013). *Foundation for Florida's Future*. Retrieved from http://www.foundationforfloridasfuture.org/Pages/About_Us/Principles.aspx.

Rado, D., & Eldeib, D. (2011, July 16). Superintendent merry-go-round yields fat severances. *Chicago Tribune*. Retrieved from http://articles.chicagotribune.com/2011-07-16/news/ct-met-superintendent-severance-20110716_1_severance-package-veteran-superintendent-board-president.

Rahm's latest union beating. (2013, April 3). *Wall Street Journal*. Retrieved from http://online.wsj.com/article/SB10001424127887324077704578358322591813256.html.

Ravitch, D. (2003). *The language police: How pressure groups restrict what students learn*. New York: Knopf.

———. (2012, February 7). Do politicians know anything at all about schools and education? Niemanwatchdog.org. Retrieved from http://www.niemanwatchdog.org/index.cfm?fuseaction=ask_this.view&askthisid=552.

Rayworth, M. (2014, July 8). Moving? How to choose the right school from afar. *ABC News*. Retrieved from http://abcnews.go.com/Health/wireStory/moving-choose-school-afar-24466375.

Reed, T. (2013, June 18). Delta, JetBlue lead airline service rankings, survey says. *TheStreet.com*. Retrieved from http://www.thestreet.com/story/11949913/1/delta-jetblue-lead-airline-service-rankings-survey-says.html.

Renaker, J. (2000). *Dr. Strangelove and the hideous epoch: Deterrence in the Nuclear Age*. Claremont, CA: Regina.

Rhetorical questions. (2013). *Silva Rhetoricae*. Retrieved from http://rhetoric.byu.edu/figures/r/rhetorical%20questions.htm.

Rhodes, J. (2007). *Framing the Black Panthers: The spectacular rise of a Black Power icon*. New York: New Press.

Rich, M. (2012, June 18). Teachers' union to open lesson-sharing web site. *New York Times*. Retrieved from http://www.nytimes.com/2012/06/19/us/teachers-union-to-open-lesson-sharing-web-site.html.

Rigertasal, L. A. (2012, Spring). Post-Watergate: The legal profession and respect for the interests of third parties. *Chapman Law Review*. Retrieved from http://www.chapmanlawreview.com/?p=62#sthash.BZH8uaIH.dpuf.

Riley, J. L. (2014, March 17). Obama's charter school rhetoric. *Wall Street Journal*. Retrieved from http://online.wsj.com/news/articles/SB10001424052702304747404579445441165698848.

Ripp, P. (2012, December 2). Should principals have term limits? *Pernilleripp.com*. Retrieved from http://www.pernilleripp.com/2012/12/should-principals-have-term-limits.html.

Rivkin, D. B., & Grossman, A. M. (2013, February 10). Gun control and the Constitution. *Wall Street Journal*. Retrieved from http://online.wsj.com/article/SB10001424127887323951904578290460073953432.html.

Robinson, S. (2013, October 2). Bowdoin College "dominated by progressive ideology," scholars say. *Maine Wire*. Retrieved from http://www.themainewire.com/2013/04/bowdoin-college-dominated-progressive-ideology-scholars.

Rose, K. D. (2001). *One nation underground: The fallout shelter in American culture*. New York: New York University Press.

Rosenberg, D. (2013, September 10). First rule of patent reform: Do no harm. *Wall Street Journal*. Retrieved from http://online.wsj.com/article/SB10001424127887324432404579053633559235404.html.

Rosenthal, B. (2012). *Are executives paid too much?* Detroit: Greenhaven.

Roth, L. (2012, October 26). NorthStar Charter's $519,000 payout to principal of failed Florida school was more than full year spent on teachers, students. *Orlando Sentinel*. Retrieved from http://www.huffingtonpost.com/2012/10/26/charter-school-spent-more_n_2021140.html.

Rotherham, A. J. (2011, February 18). The Wisconsin teachers' crisis: Who's really to blame? *Time*. Retrieved from http://www.time.com/time/nation/article/0,8599,2052705,00.html.

Rousmaniere, K. (2013, November 8). The principal: The most misunderstood person in all of education. *Atlantic*. Retrieved from http://bigeducationape.blogspot.com/2013/11/the-principal-most-misunderstood-person.html.

Rovzar, C. (2009, September 23). Mayor Bloomberg has a tortured relationship with salt. *Nymag.com*. Retrieved from http://nymag.com/daily/intelligencer/2009/09/mayor_bloomberg_has_a_tortured.html.

Roy, S. (2010). *Bomboozled: How the U.S. government misled itself and its people into believing they could survive a nuclear attack*. New York: Pointed Leaf.

Russell, J. (2013, April 10). Bowdoin president defends school after report. *Boston Globe*. Retrieved from http://www.bostonglobe.com/metro/2013/04/10/report-critiques-bowdoin-example-everything-wrong-with-liberal-arts-colleges/96ItiwuMM7NP05I2Q5VPgL/story.html.

Russolillo, S. (2013, January 10). Herbalife fights back against hedge-fund claims. *Wall Street Journal*. Retrieved from http://online.wsj.com/article/SB10001424127887324581504578233811199427712.html.

Sahlberg, P. (2011). *Finnish lessons: What can the world learn from educational change in Finland?* New York: Teachers College Press.

Salmon, F. (2012, December 31). What's Ackman's Herbalife game? *Reuters.com*. Retrieved from http://blogs.reuters.com/felix-salmon/2012/12/31/whats-ackmans-herbalife-game.

REFERENCES

Schmidt, M. S., Lipton, E., & Stevenson, A. (2014, March 9). After big bet, hedge fund pulls the levers of power. *New York Times.* Retrieved from http://www.nytimes.com/2014/03/10/business/staking-1-billion-that-herbalife-will-fail-then-ackman-lobbying-to-bring-it-down.html.

Schools seek security after Sandy Hook. (2012, December 20). *NBCNews.com.* Retrieved from http://usnews.nbcnews.com/_news/2012/12/20/16042916-armed-guards-locked-entryways-cameras-schools-seek-security-after-sandy-hook.

Schumer, C. E. (2013, June 12). A strategy for combating patent trolls. *Wall Street Journal.* Retrieved from http://online.wsj.com/article/SB10001424127887323844804578531021238656366.html.

Seidel, A. (2014, July 7). What we don't know about summer school. *nprEd.* Retrieved from http://www.npr.org/blogs/ed/2014/07/07/323659124/what-we-dont-know-about-summer-school?ft=1&f=1013.

Severson, K. (2013, September 27). Guns at school? If there's a will, there are ways. *New York Times.* Retrieved from http://www.nytimes.com/2013/09/28/us/guns-at-school-if-theres-a-will-there-are-ways.html.

Shields, C. M., & Oberg, S. L. (2000). *Year-round schooling: Promises and pitfalls.* Lanham, MD: Scarecrow.

Silver, N. (2012). *The signal and the noise: Why so many predictions fail—but some don't.* New York: Penguin.

Simon, S. (2012, August 2). Privatizing public schools: Big firms eyeing profits from U.S. K–12 market. *Huffington Post.* Retrieved from http://www.huffingtonpost.com/2012/08/02/private-firms-eyeing-prof_n_1732856.html.

Sisk, R., & Siemaszko, C. (2010, September 27). Obama suggests extending school year. *U.S. News & World Report.* Retrieved from http://www.usnews.com/news/articles/2010/09/27/obama-suggests-extending-school-year.

Slee, R., Weiner, G., & Tomlinson, S. (Eds.). (1998). *School effectiveness for whom? Challenges to the school effectiveness and school improvement movements.* London: Falmer.

Smith, A. (2013, July 3). Lululemon sued for see-through yoga pants. *CNN.com.* Retrieved from http://money.cnn.com/2013/07/03/news/companies/lululemon-yoga-lawsuit/index.html.

Smith, M. (2012, June 14). Texas schools foot big bill for STAAR retakes. *Texas Tribune.* Retrieved from http://www.texastribune.org/2012/06/14/texas-schools-foot-big-bill-staar-retakes/.

———. (2013, August 10). When charter schools are in churches, conflict is in the air. *New York Times.* Retrieved from http://www.nytimes.com/2013/08/11/us/when-charter-schools-are-in-churches-conflict-is-in-the-air.html.

———. (2014, July 10). Commitment in Texas to fiscal restraint adds burden for education. *New York Times.* Retrieved from http://www.nytimes.com/2014/07/11/us/low-education-spending-places-increased-strain-on-texas-teachers.html.

Smyth, J. C. (2013, January 13). Will longer school year help or hurt US students? *ABC News.* Retrieved from http://abcnews.go.com/US/wireStory/longer-school-year-hurt-us-students-18201500.

Snell, L. (2012). Does for-profit education meet the needs of school children: For-profit and privately managed schools benefit children in low-performing districts. In M. Young (Ed.). *For-profit education* (pp. 1–14). Detroit: Greenhaven.

Snyder, T. D. (1993). *120 years of American education: A statistical portrait.* Washington, DC: National Center for Education Statistics.

Spencer, J. (2013, February 10). Before adding time to the school day. *Education Rethink.* Retrieved from http://www.educationrethink.com/2013/02/before-adding-hours-to-day.html.

Spielman, F. (2012, October 29). 82 Chicago principals get up to $20,000 in merit bonuses. *Chicago Sun Times.* Retrieved from http://www.suntimes.com/news/metro/16035334-418/82-chicago-principals-get-up-to-20000-in-merit-bonuses.html.

Springer, J. (2010, September 27). Obama: Money without reform won't fix school system. *MSNBC.com.* Retrieved from http://today.msnbc.msn.com/id/39378576/ns/today-parenting_and_family/t/obama-money-without-reform-wont-fix-school-system.

STAAR practice test review. (2013). *Testprepreview.com.* Retrieved from http://www.testprepreview.com/staar-practice.htm.

Stamatis, B. (2009, April 2). Re-framing the public school debate. *Edwize.org.* Retrieved from http://www.edwize.org/re-framing-the-public-school-debate.

Stats about school efficiency. (2012, June 28). *Truthaboutschools.org.* Retrieved from http://www.truthaboutschools.org/2012/06/28/stats-about-school-efficiency.

Steinhauer, J. (2013, April 18). For gun bill born in tragedy, a tangled path to defeat. *New York Times.* Retrieved from http://www.nytimes.com/2013/04/19/us/tangled-birth-and-death-of-a-gun-control-bill.html.

Stepzinski, T. (2012, January 31). Duval has lowest performing high school. *Florida Times-Union.* Retrieved from http://jacksonville.com/news/florida/2012-01-30/story/state-duval-has-lowest-performing-high-school.

———. (2013, October 9). Clay School Board members say they were left in the dark about American Exceptionalism conference. *Florida Times-Union.* Retrieved from http://members.jacksonville.com/news/premium

-news/2013-10-09/story/clay-school-board-members-left-dark-about-district-partnership#.

———. (2014, July 3). Duval County Public Schools violated some laws for educating children with disabilities. *Florida Times-Union*. Retrieved from http://members.jacksonville.com/news/metro/2014-07-03/story/state-duval-county-public-schools-violated-some-laws-educating-children.

Stiles, M. (2011, March 4). Texas superintendent salaries: 2010–11. *Texas Tribune*. Retrieved from http://www.texastribune.org/library/data/texas-superintendent-salaries-2010.

Stolberg, S. G. (2013, April 2). N.R.A. details school guards plan. *New York Times*. Retrieved from http://www.nytimes.com/2013/04/03/us/nra-details-plan-for-armed-school-guards.html.

Strauss, V. (2013a, June 10). Texas governor signs legislation to reduce standardized testing. *Washington Post*. Retrieved from http://www.washingtonpost.com/blogs/answer-sheet/wp/2013/06/10/texas-governor-signs-legislation-to-reduce-standardized-testing.

———. (2013b, September 12). School named after KKK leader asked to change its name. *Washington Post*. Retrieved from http://www.washingtonpost.com/blogs/answer-sheet/wp/2013/09/12/school-named-after-kkk-leader-asked-to-change-its-name.

Strong showing in Texas house for bills to reform testing system. (2013, February 20). *Texasaftblog.com*. Retrieved from http://texasaftblog.com/hotline/?p=2565.

Stronge, J. H., Richard, H. B., & Catano, N. (2008). *Qualities of effective principals*. Alexandria, VA: Association for Supervision and Curriculum Development.

Stuit, D. A. (2010). *Are bad schools immortal?—The scarcity of turnarounds and shutdowns in both charter and district sectors*. Washington, DC: Fordham Institute.

Stutz, T. (2013, February 6). Senate votes to drop 15 percent testing rule. *Dallas News*. Retrieved from http://educationblog.dallasnews.com/2013/02/senate-votes-to-drop-15-percent-testing-rule.html.

Sullum, J. (2009, September 24). Mayor Bloomberg's salty tooth. *Reason.com*. Retrieved from http://reason.com/blog/2009/09/24/mayor-bloombergs-salty-tooth.

Suskie, L. A. (2009). *Assessing student learning: A common sense guide*. San Francisco, CA: Jossey-Bass.

Swaim, B. (2014, January 14). In defense of political obfuscation. *Wall Street Journal*. Retrieved from http://online.wsj.com/news/articles/SB10001424052702303933104579307191443290038.

Swasey, C. (2013, June 13). My view: Common Core an assault on liberties. *Deseret News*. Retrieved from http://www.deseretnews.com/article/765632044/Common-Core-an-assault-on-liberties.html.

Symonds, W. C., Palmer, A. T., Lindorff, D., & McCann, J. (2000, February 7). For-profit schools. *Businessweek*. Retrieved from http://www.businessweek.com/2000/00_06/b3667001.htm.

Tavernise, S. (2014, June 13). Controlling the message in Ukraine. *New York Times*. Retrieved from http://www.nytimes.com/2014/06/15/sunday-review/controlling-the-message-in-ukraine.html.

Taylor, R. (2013, February 19). Teachers with guns, allowed under proposed new law. *NBCNews.com*. Retrieved from http://www.nbcnews.com/id/50853163/ns/local_news-tucson_az.

Texas STAAR: Your source for STAAR tutorial materials. (2013). *TripleNterprises Publishing*. Retrieved from http://www.txstaar.com.

Texas textbooks: What happened, what it means, and what we can do about it. (2010, June 18). *People for the American Way*. Retrieved from http://www.pfaw.org/rww-in-focus/texas-textbooks-what-happened-what-it-means-and-what-we-can-do-about-it.

Thinking about a virtual school? (2013). *Calvert Education Services*. Retrieved from http://duvalvirtualk5.org/landing/dvia.

Thompson, E. (2013, June 24). Gators basketball recruit Chris Walker facing academic eligibility issues. *Florida Times-Union*. Retrieved from http://jacksonville.com/sports/college/florida-gators/2013-06-24/story/gators-basketball-recruit-chris-walker-facing.

Thurman, T. (2014, January 20). Is Common Core really state-led? *The Daily Signal*. Retrieved from http://dailysignal.com/2014/01/20/common-core-really-state-led.

Top ten problems with the STAAR Test. (2013). *Save Texas Schools*. Retrieved from http://savetxschools.org/too-many-tests/top-ten-problems-with-the-staar-test.

Travis, S. (2013, March 7). State report: Florida charter schools outperform traditional schools. *SunSentinel*. Retrieved from http://articles.sun-sentinel.com/2013-03-07/news/sfl-charter-school-report-20130307_1_charter-school-students-achievement-gap-student-achievement.

Turner, C. (2014, June 3). The common core curriculum void. *nprEd*. Retrieved from http://www.npr.org/blogs/ed/2014/06/03/318228023/the-common-core-curriculum-void?ft=1&f=1013.

Union concerned about bonuses for principals. (2012, March 25). *WA Today*. Retrieved from http://www.watoday.com.au/wa-news/union-concerned-about-bonuses-for-principals-20120325-1vs0y.html.

REFERENCES

United States Subcommittee on Elementary, Secondary, and Vocational Education. (1991, July 25). *Hearing on perspectives on extending the school year.* Washington, DC: Government Printing Office.

Utah teachers get free gun training in response to Newtown shooting. (2012, December 28). *NBCNews.com.* Retrieved from http://usnews.nbcnews.com/_news/2012/12/28/16206006-utah-teachers-get-free-gun-training-in-response-to-newtown-shooting.

Villaraigosa, A. (2014, July 20). Why are teachers unions so opposed to change? *Wall Street Journal.* Retrieved from http://online.wsj.com/articles/antonio-villaraigosa-why-are-teachers-unions-so-opposed-to-change-1405893828.

Watters, A. (2011, July 25). How data and analytics can improve education. *O'Reilly Radar.* Retrieved from http://strata.oreilly.com/2011/07/education-data-analytics-learning.html.

Weigley, S. (2011, October 6). Have CEO severance packages gotten out of hand? *International Business Times.* Retrieved from http://www.ibtimes.com/have-ceo-severance-packages-gotten-out-hand-321726.

What to do when there is a problem with the principal. (2013). *Great Schools.* Retrieved from http://www.greatschools.org/improvement/quality-teaching/5-what-to-do-when-there-is-a-problem-with-the-principal.gs.

Whatever means necessary. (2012, July 29). *Wall Street Journal.* Retrieved from http://online.wsj.com/article/SB10000872396390444860104577557001406123724.html.

Whiteside, K. (2013, May 28). Rutgers alumni forced to deal with more controversy. *USA TODAY.* Retrieved from http://www.usatoday.com/story/sports/college/2013/05/28/rutgers-athletic-director-julie-hermann-mike-rice/2367335.

Will analytics transform education? (2013). *Learning Frontiers.* Retrieved from http://www.learningfrontiers.eu/?q=story/will-analytics-transform-education.

Will Obama's budget recognize charter schools? (2013, March 26). *Wall Street Journal.* Retrieved from http://online.wsj.com/article/SB10001424127887324557804578376301012270328.html.

Williams, J. (2012, February 28). Will business boost school reform? *Wall Street Journal.* Retrieved from http://online.wsj.com/article/SB10001424052970204520204577249081544142106.html.

Wyatt, E. (2013, July 16). F.T.C. turns a lens on abusers of the patent system. *New York Times.* Retrieved from http://www.nytimes.com/2013/07/17/business/ftc-turns-a-lens-on-abusers-of-the-patent-system.html.

Yaccino, S. (2013, July 7). Schools seeking to arm employees hit hurdle on insurance. *New York Times.* Retrieved from http://www.nytimes.com/2013/07/08/us/schools-seeking-to-arm-employees-hit-hurdle-on-insurance.html.

Young, M. (Ed.). (2012). *For-profit education*. Detroit: Greenhaven.

Zernike, K. (2012, August 6). Christie signs bill overhauling job guarantees for teachers. *New York Times*. Retrieved from http://www.nytimes.com/2012/08/07/nyregion/christie-signs-bill-overhauling-teacher-tenure.html.

Zimmer, J. (2012, January 25). Rhetorical devices: Hypophora. *Manner of Speaking*. Retrieved from http://mannerofspeaking.org/2012/01/25/rhetorical-devices-hypophora.

ABOUT THE AUTHOR

Gerard Giordano is a professor at the University of North Florida. He has written more than a dozen books, including *Solving Education's Problems Effectively, Cockeyed Education, Lopsided Schools, Capping Costs, Teachers Go to Rehab,* and *Commonsense Questions about Instruction.* His recent books were published by Rowman & Littlefield Education.

www.ingramcontent.com/pod-product-compliance
Lightning Source LLC
Chambersburg PA
CBHW051812230426
43672CB00012B/2708